Life Advice That Doesn't Suck!

365 simple ways to live a more satisfying life

Jeremy Godwin

A Reconnaissance Media publication

Copyright information

Life Advice That Doesn't Suck!

365 simple ways to live a more satisfying life

First edition November 2022

ISBN: 978-0-6456633-1-0 (print)
ISBN: 978-0-6456633-0-3 (ebook)

Published by Reconnaissance Media
www.reconnaissancemedia.com

"Joy is not in things; it is in us."

Richard Wagner (1813-1883)

Introduction

Let's face it, some life advice just sucks. "Don't worry, be happy"? What the hell is that?!

Anyone prone to worry and overthinking knows that the absolute *worst* thing someone can say to you is to just stop worrying. How are you supposed to respond to that, "Oh wow, thanks Bill, I never thought of that!" (and feel free to insert an eye roll while you're saying it, if you really want to up the sass-factor!)?

Back in 2021 I had a random idea to start posting the odd bit of life advice that *didn't* suck; tips that were blunt, honest and thought-provoking while also being balanced and with a focus on what is best for creating good mental health and wellbeing. I tend to be quite direct in my weekly podcast, *Let's Talk About Mental Health*, and most people seem to respond well to me being blunt so these posts were about allowing me to share some of the tips I give in the podcast in a short and quick way, rather than making you listen to a full 25-minute podcast episode full of how-to information.

I began posting them intermittently on my @jeremygodwinofficial account on Instagram, which then grew to doing daily posts from the start of 2022 onwards, and I really love hearing back from people who have found my tips helpful and highly relevant to something they're dealing with in their life at the time.

These tips tend to come to me at random moments, and I'll often find that I'm in the middle of doing something and have to quickly grab my phone to make a note before I forget whatever piece of advice just popped into my head out of nowhere (so if you ever see me in the supermarket tapping away intensely at my phone, now you know what I'm probably doing; either that, or I'm looking at a meme my friend sent me about cats or weird fashion…).

You may not always agree with my tips, but the point is to challenge you to think about yourself —

and the world — a little differently, and to find the tips that work for you which help you to push yourself out of your comfort zone in order to grow. Why? Because when you grow, you learn how to focus less of your energy and attention on the stuff that doesn't matter and more on the stuff that *does* matter… because that's what helps you to feel more satisfied in your life, and that's *always* a good thing!

Oh, and why did I end up calling it *Life Advice That Doesn't Suck*? Because a lot of so-called advice really does suck! Have you seen half of the nonsense spouted by so-called self-help 'experts' who have no actual lived experience of the thing they're talking about? It absolutely annoys the hell out of me! Look, the thing is that I'm not telling you anything in this book that I wouldn't do myself, and I will not tell you anything that's going to make life more complicated… life really is complex enough.

I believe in creating and maintaining balance and simplicity in your life above all things, and that's the core of what I talk about in my work as a writer, podcaster, counsellor and coach (I do a lot of things). And a quick word here about simplicity: 'simple' rarely means 'easy', because creating simplicity actually requires you to let go of a lot of the ideas you've had for a long time about who you should be and what you should do with your life, and that's hard work… but it's worth it. It's a topic I discuss over and over again in my podcast and in my books, so please check them out if you'd like to explore the idea of simplicity and better mental health in more detail.

A final note: I've presented this book in mostly the same order as I posted these on Instagram which means that you'll see my tips progressively increase in length as you work your way through the book. This is a reflection of where I began to experiment more with using video and carousel posts to deliver greater information, so entries in the second half of the book are longer than the first.

I hope you enjoy my *Life Advice That Doesn't Suck* and that you find it helpful. Let me know on Instagram which ones resonated the most with you, and feel free to share some of your own!

Jeremy Godwin

October 2022, Australia

1. Focus on one day at a time.

What if?...

Choose to focus on one day at a time. ~~Why?~~

Because you cannot predict what tomorrow may bring… and besides, you live here in the present so really *live* here in the present.

2. Your future is whatever you make it.

You are the one in control of your future, by means of the choices you make or don't make… so create the future you want, one step at a time.

3. It's never too late to try something new.

You are not too old, too late, too 'past it'… try something new. The only time it's ever too late is after you have left this life. Never let age hold you back from doing all the things that you've always wanted to.

4. The purpose of life is to live a purposeful life.

When you have a sense of purpose, you become determined to achieve whatever it is that you are most passionate about and what helps you to feel fulfilled, and that makes life feel more joyful.

5. Choose to be the best version of yourself possible.

You get to choose what you do and say, so choose to be the best version of yourself possible each and every day… that helps you to grow and it keeps you focused on positivity and kindness. It doesn't mean that you won't make mistakes (you will), but it will help you to set positively-focused intentions so that you can operate from a place of kindness.

6. Mistakes are only failures if you don't learn from them.

It's OK to make mistakes; the main thing is to learn from them. A mistake is only a failure if you don't learn the lesson so that you can grow from whatever happened.

7. You are not in competition with anyone but yourself.

Every single one of us is unique, so there's no point comparing yourself to others or trying to compete with people who are different to you; that's what we call 'comparing apples with oranges'. Focus on you and you alone, and aim each day to be a little better than you were the day before.

8. It's OK to stop interacting with people who make you feel bad about yourself.

You get to choose who has access to you. No amount of effort on your part will ever change another person; only they can choose whether or not to change. If they choose to be hurtful and do harm to you, choose to limit their access to you or walk away entirely.

9. Choose to grow.

Growth is a choice. Change will always go on around you and within you, and you can either resist it (and cause yourself suffering) or learn to accept it so that you can grow. Guess which one is the healthier option?!

10. Not all friendships are meant to last, and that's OK.

I wish I could tell you that all of your friendships will last for forever; some might, but not all of them will… and that's OK. Some relationships are more about who you were at that stage in your life. Celebrate the positives you took from the friendship, and let it go with grace and dignity.

11. Just because someone is related to you, that doesn't give them the right to treat you poorly.

Being family doesn't give someone a free pass to treat you terribly. This is, sadly, one of several life lessons I have had to learn over and over again. There's a very clear line between being kind and putting up with rubbish. Do not put up with rubbish, especially when it's damaging to your mental health.

12. You are not the same person you were yesterday.

Growth is a wonderful thing, because you are never the same person from one day to the next. The choices you make today shape who you are becoming, so celebrate that and challenge yourself to make thoughtful choices that help you to grow a little each day.

13. There is no going back.

As hard as it is to hear this, you need to accept this simple fact of life: you cannot go back. You cannot ever un-know what you have learned. You cannot change the past. Learn what you need to learn and move forward.

14. Life is change, regardless of whether we like it or not.

You can resist change all you like, but that won't stop it from happening. Instead of fighting it, choose to embrace it. That doesn't mean you have to like it; it simply means you understand how futile it is to fight against something you have no control over. Instead, turn your focus to what you *do* have control over: your words and actions.

15. Even terrible days only last for 24 hours.

When you take things one day at a time, one step at a time, it becomes easier to make your way through the tough days... because a day is just 24 hours long.

16. Do what makes you happy.

There are so many expectations that we face from family, friends and society in general... just be you and do what you do. If it doesn't harm anyone (including yourself) and it makes you happy, who cares what other people think?!

17. Don't try to fit in; instead, find your niche.

When I was younger, I spent *so* long trying to fit in that I lost my sense of self. Embrace who you are and be 100% you, and you will find your people. Anyone who doesn't like you for you is not one of your people.

18. True beauty comes from authenticity.

When you are true to yourself, your inner beauty shines brighter than any diamond. Be yourself, always.

19. Nurture your soul above all things.

Beauty comes from within. There is no point putting a massive amount of effort into how you look if you're not going to take the time to nurture your soul, because true beauty comes from your soul.

20. Rest is not an indulgence, it's a basic necessity.

You cannot run at full speed non-stop, so make regular time for quality rest and relaxation. Without it you will not be able to function effectively long-term.

21. If you don't look after yourself, nobody is going to do it for you.

Even the people who care most about you in the world cannot look after you physically and mentally, because only you can do that. So... do that! Nobody can or will do it for you.

22. When in doubt, simplify.

Given a choice between complexity and simplicity, you'll usually find that the simplest option will make life easier in the long-term.

23. What you focus on is what you focus on.

Where your attention goes, energy flows... so be mindful of how the way you look at the world is influencing your focus.

24. It's OK to remove toxic influences from your life (actually, it's recommended).

If you saw that some food or drink was labelled 'toxic', would you eat or drink it? No? So why then do you tolerate toxic people in your life?! Toxic equals bad for you. Walk away (and definitely do *not* consume!).

25. Your parents are just people, and nobody is perfect.

It's easy to put huge expectations on our parents to be everything we need them to be, but they're just people and we're all imperfect. That doesn't give them a free pass, but it does serve to remind you to be objective.

26. All storms eventually pass.

No matter how dark the skies might be at the moment, they will eventually clear. That applies to weather and it applies to your life. All storms eventually pass, and you will be OK.

27. Follow your heart.

When faced with a choice, consider what your heart is telling you... because that is your soul speaking to you. All decisions need to be grounded in rational thought, but your heart plays a massive role too.

28. It's OK to completely change your life.

Life is change and if that means that you want to or need to completely change your life, do it. It's your life.

29. Nobody has all the answers.

I wish I could tell you that I have it all figured out, but I don't. Nobody does. And that's OK. Life is about figuring it all out one day at a time, and that is something you will be doing for the rest of your life... so enjoy the process!

30. You matter to somebody.

Sometimes we can get caught up in negative emotions or find ourselves feeling down due to issues with other people, but never forget that you matter to somebody (and I'd wager that you matter to a lot of somebodies).

31. You do not have to be perfect to be whole (besides, 'perfect' doesn't exist).

I hate to break this to you, but you will never be perfect. Which isn't a bad thing... can you imagine how incredibly dull and boring life would be if we didn't have any growing to do?! Stop expecting yourself to be perfect, because that's an unattainable goal which just sets you up for failure. Just focus on being the best you can be today, and growing a little every day.

32. Never let other people's judgements stop you from being your true self.

There will always be people who choose to force their opinions onto others and who think that they, and only they, have figured out the one single correct way to live... they haven't, because nobody has all the answers. Leave them to their delusions and don't let them stop you from being 100% authentic.

33. There are plenty of unkind people in the world... don't be one of them.

Choose not to let yourself be deliberately unkind to others. There are enough unkind people in the world, and since you get to choose what you say and do that means you can choose to be kind. Spread kindness like pixie dust, because you get back what you put out.

34. The things other people do are about them, not you.

We're often convinced that other people are focused on us as much as we are... but they're not. Every single person on this planet is mainly focused on themselves, and I *guarantee* you most of them also think you're scrutinising them as much as they are themselves. When you know and embrace that, it makes it easier to care less about what others think (because they really are thinking about you much, *much* less than what you think they are).

35. In all things you have choice.

In any given situation, whether internal or external, you have choice. Even not making a choice is a choice.

36. All you have direct control over is yourself, and what you choose to do and say.

When I finally accepted that what other people do and say is completely out of my control, I found peace. I also found the strength to walk away from people who were never going to change.

37. Unhealthy coping mechanisms lead to unhealthy outcomes.

Look, I don't want to be THAT person... but I'm going to be: you can't expect to have healthy outcomes from unhealthy actions. It's annoying, but it's true…

38. Positivity breeds positivity.

The more you see the positives in life, the more positives you will see. And always remember that your mindset is a choice (which I discussed in Episode 31 of my podcast, *Let's Talk About Mental Health*).

39. What you consume, physically and mentally, creates your reality.

What goes in creates your reality... so consume thoughtfully. That means being mindful of what you put in your body and what you put in your mind. A diet of little else but refined sugar and non-stop news channels will eventually do a lot of damage to you.

40. Be who you want to be.

Why would you spend your life trying to be something (or someone) that you're not? BE YOU! If what you're doing isn't harming anyone or yourself, go for it and make the most out of your life. It's your life!

41. Be curious.

Remember the joy and wonder you felt as a kid? Rediscover that! Look at the world with curiosity, and resolve to be more joyful.

42. Create.

The word 'create' may seem like a small one but it's actually enormous; everything that is, ever was, and ever will be was once just an idea in someone's mind which they then created. Allow your imagination to flow and tap into that part of yourself that wants to do something creative. There are so many different ways you can create, so sit with the idea of it for a little while and consider what your heart is telling you.

43. Learn a little every day.

When you learn a little each day, you stimulate your mind and you find new ideas that help you to look at the world in a different way. Learning is growth, and growth is essential so that you don't stagnate.

44. Your wellbeing has to come first.

You have to look after yourself, because nobody can or will take do it for you. Even the people that you love you the most cannot 'fix' your mental and emotional ouchies and boo-boos; only you can do that. Make your wellbeing your top priority.

45. Speak less, listen more.

You have two ears and one mouth, so use them in that ratio and listen more than you speak. You learn more when you listen more.

46. Set boundaries and maintain them.

It's up to you to set your boundaries and communicate them. Guess what? Other people cannot guess your boundaries; you have to tell them and/or show them. And then you need to stick to them.

47. A boundary that is not enforced is just an imaginary line.

Enforce your boundaries. I mean, I'm not saying that you have to erect a fence and post guards at regular intervals... but don't call it a boundary if you're not going to actually enforce it if or when it is breached.

48. You are not your job title.

Your job is what you do, not who you are. Hear that again: your job is what you do, *not* who you are.

49. Self-awareness allows you to respond to things more thoughtfully.

When you know yourself, you can more readily identify emotional reactions as they are happening so that you can pause, observe them, release them and then respond in a more thoughtful and considered way… which leads to far fewer misunderstandings and issues.

50. Change is going to happen whether you accept it or not.

The one thing we can *all* guarantee is that life is change, and the world will keep on spinning regardless of our efforts to stop it. Instead of fighting it, embrace change and embrace growth.

51. You won't get all the answers you're hoping for from others, and that's OK.

'Closure' is not a given; very often you just won't find the answers you're hoping for. Make your peace with that so you can make your peace with whatever happened or didn't happen.

52. Healing takes work.

There are no short-cuts when it comes to healing and no magic pills you can take; healing takes time, effort and perseverance. But it *is* possible.

53. Maturity doesn't automatically come with age.

Your age is not a predictor of your maturity level; I know some older people who behave like absolute children. Maturity is a choice, and it's a sign of personal growth.

54. You are not your mistakes, you are what you do with them.

No matter how hard you try not to, you are going to make mistakes in life. Learn from them and see them as an opportunity to grow. They do not define you unless you let them. I have made *so* many mistakes in my life, but without them I wouldn't be where I am — or who I am — today.

55. It's never too late for a fresh start.

You can always start again. *Always*. It's never too late to try something new or head in a different direction… it's your life, so live it!

56. If your job is making you miserable, it's time to leave. Nothing is worth that.

There's a huge difference between being a bit 'meh' about your job versus feeling completely and utterly miserable about it. 'Miserable' is unacceptable. Anything that makes you feel miserable has to go.

57. Anything that costs you your peace of mind is too expensive.

I have learned to value my peace of mind above all things, and it has changed my life for the better. Anything (or anyone) that detracts from that just isn't worth it.

58. Your batteries need to be recharged regularly.

You can try to keep on going and going and going without a break, but sooner or later you're going to run out of juice. Make time every day to reset, recharge and replenish. You cannot operate at 100% non-stop… you're human, not a robot.

59. Start something new.

Because if you keep on doing the same thing over and again, then you're not growing… and growth is the thing that helps you to be a little better every day, and new things create new possibilities in your life.

60. Do one thing each day that terrifies you.

Fear can often hold us back from trying new things or addressing challenges, but you are the one in control of what happens next… so instead of letting fear control you, choose to control it. Nothing ventured, nothing gained!

61. Relationships require work.

The fairytale ending of 'living happily ever after' is a lie, because all relationships change and evolve over time… just as you do. Do the work and communicate openly and often.

62. New beginnings are often disguised as endings.

Endings are often sad and painful, but at the same time they create space for the new. The fact is that life is change, and nothing lasts forever; mourn the loss but celebrate what was, rather than fixating on the loss, so you can move forward.

63. Treat yourself with respect.

Because, frankly, if you don't treat yourself with respect then how can you expect other people to?! Be kind to yourself and learn how to celebrate your strengths while also challenging yourself to grow a little each day, so you can continue to evolve.

64. Never let someone else treat you with disrespect.

This one is fairly self-explanatory: **never** let someone else treat you with disrespect, because what you allow is what you get. If someone is disrespecting you, remember that you deserve better and you don't have to put up with crap.

65. It takes work to turn your dreams into reality.

If you want to make something happen then do the work. You can make all the wishes you like, but unless you take action nothing will happen. Break down what you want to achieve into small chunks and make progress one day at a time, one step at a time.

66. Don't over-engineer things... the simpler, the better.

We so often make life more difficult for ourselves than it needs to be. Here's my approach to most things: if it matters, then I focus on it, and if it doesn't matter, then it doesn't matter. Keep it simple.

67. Take calculated risks in life.

If you never try new things then you never make any progress, but at the same time you don't want to just jump off every bridge you come across. Take the time to make thoughtful decisions that balance risk and reward.

68. When it comes to friends, quality is more important than quantity.

When it comes to friendship, what matters most is having people who you can be your true self with and vice versa… it doesn't matter how many. Know the difference between 'friends' and 'acquaintances'.

69. Life is an experiment; you have to figure it out for yourself.

We don't get handed an instruction manual when we're born, which is why so many people try to project their view of what is right or wrong onto others. We're all just figuring things out as we go along, so choose to be your own person.

70. The bad news is that only you can change you. The good news is that only you can change you.

Nobody can change you; they can influence you, sure, but they cannot actually change you… only you can do that. Which means you get to create your life the way that feels right for you.

71. What you do today matters more than what you did or didn't do yesterday.

Every day you get to reinvent yourself, and the fact of life is that none of us is perfect and we all have a history. Instead of focusing on who you were, learn from that and celebrate who you are becoming each day.

72. It's the daily habits that shape your future, not the things you just do sometimes.

Things you do infrequently will have little long-term impact; it's the stuff you do every day, or most days, which shapes your reality, so choose your habits wisely.

73. Define success for yourself, instead of basing it on what everyone else tells you it should look like.

The great philosopher, Madonna, was right when she said you don't need diamond rings or eighteen karat gold. Decide what success looks like for you and don't worry about other peoples' opinions.

74. To be happy with yourself you need to look within yourself, not towards others.

Other people can never and will never complete you… only you can do that, so look within.

75. You cannot control what happens, but you *can* control how you respond to what happens.

There will always be things that go on around you or in the wider world that are completely out of your control, and you can get hung up on that stuff or you can focus on what is within your own control; in other words, your words and actions along with what you do with your feelings. That's how you find peace of mind.

76. No matter how hard you might try, you cannot make someone like you or love you.

The choices other people make are out of your control. If someone isn't responding the way you want them to, express your needs and then if they don't respect that it means they're not the right person for you, and that's OK. It's healthier to accept the truth and move forward with your dignity and self-respect intact.

77. Stop trying to control the things that are out of your control.

You can either put all of your energy and attention into the things going on around you, which is the stuff you cannot directly control, or you can accept what is out of your control and get on with you *can* control; in other words, yourself and what you choose to do or not do. Focusing on what you can control, instead of what you cannot, is the quickest way to find peace of mind.

78. Kindness leads to happiness.

When you are kind to others, they are more likely to be kind back to you… it's like a circle of love. And when you're kind to yourself, you feel better about yourself. Kindness for the win!

79. Be honest.

Honesty might create challenges (because the truth can be uncomfortable or confronting), but it's significantly better than the mess left behind by deception. A lot of misunderstandings happen because we're afraid of conflict, or we don't want to hurt someone's feelings, but it's better to be honest (with kindness) than to be dishonest. Make your choice.

80. Small changes add up to create big results.

Don't try to do everything all at once. Instead, break things down into their smallest possible steps and make progress little by little; it's easier to achieve, and much more sustainable in the long term.

81. Self care is self respect.

When you look after yourself and treat yourself with kindness, you are saying "I am worthy and I matter" — which you do. And as I've said many times before, if you don't look after yourself then who will?

82. It's OK not to have everything figured out yet.

I guarantee you that every single person on this planet is just making it all up as they go along, myself included! Nobody has all the answers and there is no timeline on when you have to have it all worked out. Take things one day at a time and focus on growing a little each day.

83. Gratitude helps you to see all the wonderful things in your life.

The more you are grateful for, the more you discover to be grateful for… and that's a pretty solid return on investment! Even during the toughest of times, there is always something to be grateful for.

84. Sometimes the question <u>is</u> the answer.

If you're not sure about something or someone and you can't seem to find an answer to your questions, then perhaps the question itself actually *is* the answer… because if you feel uncertain, that might be telling you exactly what you need to know.

85. Your only competition is yourself.

You're in a race of one: you, and you alone. Every single one of us is unique, so instead of comparing yourself to others choose to focus on growing a little every day.

86. If you can't be kind, at least don't be nasty.

Honestly, I don't understand why so many people choose to pump out toxic comments online or in-person when all that does is create more toxicity. If you don't like something, don't comment! Not every opinion needs to be shared.

87. Love is all.

When it all boils down to it, what matters most in life is love in all of its many beautiful forms… and that means with others (whether platonic or romantic) as well as with yourself. Choose love above all things.

88. Truth is priceless.

I'd much prefer to know exactly where I stand with other people than be fed what they think I want to hear. Sure, the truth might hurt sometimes, but it's far better in the long-run than deception. Be truthful with others and ask them to be truthful with you.

89. Your way of doing things is not the only way.

There are many different ways to do the same type of thing, and they're all valid; don't try to enforce your ideals and approaches onto others. Instead, you do what you do and let them do what they do. If it isn't harming anyone, it's nobody's business. Oh, and I encourage you to also learn about different ways of doing things because that's how you expand your mind… which is how you grow.

90. The point of life is to live.

That means changing, growing, evolving… and you do that by trying new things and being open to new ideas. If nothing changes then nothing changes.

91. Winning isn't everything.

Being proud of the work you did and the effort you put in is what matters most in life, and even if it doesn't work out as you had hoped then remember that it's still a learning experience.

92. Try new things, and if it doesn't work then try something else.

Don't worry about whether or not something will fail… try anyway. It's better to try than to never know, and if you decide you don't want to continue then you can always change your mind.

93. We all fail sometimes.

It's what you do with the failure that matters more than whatever did or didn't happen. A failure is simply a learning opportunity in disguise.

94. If you have to force it, it's not going to work.

You can't make someone give you love and affection, and you can't make a difficult relationship or situation magically turn into a great one by pushing it. If it feels like it's wrong, then it's probably wrong.

95. If you're tired, rest.

It's not possible to run at 100% forever, and if your body and soul are telling you to slow down then slow down. You're not going to miss out and in fact you'll be more productive as a result of recharging your energy.

96. How someone treats you matters more than how much you like them.

We can often give people a free pass for the way they treat us because we like them, but all that does is reinforce that it's OK to treat you poorly. It's not. It's *really* not. Be assertive and direct, ask for what you need, and don't settle for second best just because you like someone.

97. Learn how to like yourself.

Spend less time worrying about what other people think of you and more time learning how to be someone that you actually like, because if you don't like yourself then you tend to do and say things that are out of alignment with who you truly are.

98. You don't have to decide on the rest of your life today.

For some reason we expect ourselves (and others) to pick a specific life path or career field and stick to it, and that's actually pretty weird. As we learn and grow we become different versions of ourselves, and our priorities change and evolve over time. I think it's wiser to focus on what you're drawn to now, in this phase of your life, and give yourself permission to change your mind if you want to try something else later. Who cares what other people think? It's your life!

99. Don't change yourself just to fit in.

The fact is that there will always be people who don't like you, regardless of what you do or say, so why would you waste your energy trying to be something or someone that you're not? Fitting in is overrated! Instead, be true to yourself and, over time, you'll find plenty of people who like you for you (plus, you'll feel a lot better about yourself because you're being authentic).

100. 'Be yourself' doesn't mean 'be rude'.

Treat other people with kindness and respect (even if that isn't what they're giving back to you) and remember that you can be true to yourself without being horrible to people. If you can't agree with someone or find common ground, walk away… because what you put out into the world shapes the world around you, so choose kindness.

101. You can disagree without having an argument.

It's up to you whether or not you choose to turn a disagreement into an argument, and frankly arguing is fairly pointless; when heated emotions get involved, we rarely listen to one another. You can choose to simply say "I disagree," and leave it at that.

102. Choose to see the good in your life.

Focus on what is good in your life at this moment. Why? Because what we focus on is what we focus on, so the more you focus on the negative the more negative stuff you will find to focus on… whereas when you focus on the positive, you'll find even more to feel positively about. That doesn't mean that you should just pretend everything is perfect (because that's delusion), but it means you learn how to celebrate the good in spite of your challenges, which helps you to find greater satisfaction in your life.

103. You can choose what to do with your thoughts.

You know those thoughts that go through your head sometimes telling you that you're not good enough or that you're a failure? You get to decide whether or not to listen to them. Oh, and by the way… those thoughts are not true.

104. Be grateful for what you have now, today.

If you're constantly focused on what is next and trying to do, be and get more, more, more, then you're missing out on all of the wonderful things already in your life now. You don't live in the world of tomorrow; you live here, today… so *live* here, today.

105. Some people just aren't for you.

You're never going to get along with everybody and that's OK; you get to choose who has access to you, so if someone isn't for you then limit their access to you or remove it entirely.

106. Keep your standards high and your expectations low.

Instead of hoping that people will behave a certain way towards you, be clear on your standards and set your boundaries accordingly while also communicating what you need. That leads to far less disappointment.

107. Sometimes you need to choose between attention and peace of mind.

It can be all-too-easy to fall into a trap of wanting to be seen and valued by someone who is never going to be able to truly meet your needs. Value your peace of mind above all things, and if you're not being treated decently then choose to prioritise your self worth.

108. All that you are and all that you will ever be is determined by your choices.

Whatever you decide to do or not do will shape what happens next. That can be a bit overwhelming to think about at first, but it actually serves to remind you that you are the one in control of your own destiny based on the choices you make or don't make. That is true power.

109. Don't ever let someone else tell you who you are.

Only you can ever truly know what is in your heart, so when you follow along with someone else's expectations of who or what you should be you will inevitably create pain and disappointment for yourself. Be 100% yourself. You can do that in a way that is kind, respectful and which does no harm to others or yourself.

110. You get the future you create today.

There are big ticket events that influence our life, but for the most part it's the little things that you do and say each day which will shape your future. If you want to create change, then begin with one small change and slowly shift things over time… because small steps add up to enormous results.

111. Being alive is a privilege.

The fact that you woke up today and get to experience life in all of its many shapes and forms is pretty damn amazing! And if you have the opportunity to do it again tomorrow, that's even more amazing! Celebrate each and every day, and remember how fortunate you are.

112. Endings are also beginnings.

Processing loss and grief is one of the hardest things we have to do as human beings, but it's inevitable. Change is constant and change is painful. But from even the most painful of times, new things are created.

113. Satisfaction is creating a life for yourself that doesn't require you to find distractions.

You're never going to have a perfect life, because 'perfect' doesn't exist. But when you build a foundation for yourself based on the stuff that brings you deep satisfaction, it becomes less necessary to try and distract yourself from your life with unhealthy habits and behaviours.

114. Make time for those you care about.

What matters most to you in this life? My guess is that, for most of you, highest on your list will be the people closest to you; the people you care about the most. So, if that's the case, that immediately tells you how you should be spending the majority of your time. Focus on what *really* matters, and let everything else be background noise.

115. Own your choices.

You're never going to get it right all of the time; I've made some monumental mistakes in my life, as I'm sure you have, and that's just a part of growth. Take ownership of the choices you make and if you mess up, treat it as a learning opportunity so that you can do better in the future.

116. Kindness beats hatred.

Did your parents or guardians ever tell you that 'two wrongs don't make a right'? In other words, that meeting unkindness with more unkindness does nothing but multiply it? Even in the face of outright hatred, choose to walk away rather than stooping to their level.

117. If it doesn't harm others or yourself, do what brings you joy.

It really doesn't matter what other people think about your choices; I mean, to be fair, other people will never agree with you 100% of the time anyway… so who cares what they think?! If you aren't harming anyone (including yourself) and it makes you feel joyful, then you do you.

118. Unhealthy habits lead to unhealthy outcomes.

This is one of those boring bits of advice that you probably want to roll your eyes over but I'm going to say it anyway because it's a fact: your little habits add up over time to create your reality, so those unhealthy choices can grow into a much bigger issue if left unaddressed. Think carefully, and focus on consciously building healthy habits.

119. Don't be cruel.

In a world where it seems like there are so many people ready and willing to be cruel and hateful to others, especially when they don't agree with who they are or how they live their lives, don't go and add more fuel to the fire… because not only does that just create a bigger fire, it also does harm to others and to your own wellbeing. Be kind.

120. Give the gift of your time to those who will value it most.

Under no circumstances should you keep on giving and giving to people who don't appreciate and value you, because that eats away at your soul. Instead, focus your energy towards the people who value you and who lift you up because that's how you live a life that feels more satisfying. Life is about a healthy balance of give and take.

121. Make your wellbeing a priority every day.

The boring fact is that only you can look after your own wellbeing… so, if you want to feel better then it's up to you to do the work! That means looking after all the different areas of your wellbeing: physical, mental, spiritual, social, emotional and financial. And it also means remembering that your wellbeing is more important than whatever it is that you do for work; jobs come and go, but your health is precious.

122. Learn something new every day.

You don't stop learning and growing just because you reach a certain age or because you have a piece of paper from a university; learning is a lifelong process, and there's so much to discover. Approach every day with a sense of curiosity and wonder.

123. The most important relationship you will ever have is the one you have with yourself.

Other people may come and go from your life, but you are going to be with you for the rest of your life… so why not make that a healthy and positive relationship? After all, if you don't treat yourself well then how can you expect others to?!

124. Know what your priorities are and focus on them.

There will always be a million different tasks and shiny objects trying to compete for your attention, but most of them really don't matter in the big scheme of things. Take time to understand what (or who) your main 3-5 priorities are in life and give them the bulk of your attention, because *that* is what really matters — not all the other noise and drama.

125. A healthy relationship involves balance.

Relationships are great, but they have to be mutually rewarding to be healthy; finding that balance takes time and, more importantly, it takes work. There is no magic 'happy ever after' for relationships; even fairytale characters probably had an argument about the dishes every now and then, and that's OK!

126. Choose not to speak or act in anger.

Anger can be a positive thing, because it shows us what we feel intensely about, however if you just react out of anger without thinking then you can easily create chaos. Instead, choose to consciously pause and wait a few seconds to let your logical brain catch up with your emotions so that you can respond in a more thoughtful and considered way.

127. Don't try to be perfect, just be decent.

Look, 'perfect' really doesn't exist; every single one of us has flaws and things that we could be better at, but I think that's the whole point; our journey in life is about discovering who we are, flaws and all, and then figuring out how to be a decent person in spite of all of our baggage (and that means that you do no harm, be kind and give more than you take).

128. Ignorance is not bliss.

It's easy to fall into a trap of thinking that we know everything but the reality is that most of us are like Jon Snow from *Game of Thrones*: we know nothing. The more you learn, the more you realise how little you actually know… which is exciting, because you can always learn more! Choose to learn instead of choosing ignorance, because we really don't need more ignorance in this world.

129. Be kind to yourself.

There are enough mean-spirited people in the world… don't choose to behave that way towards yourself! Learn how to love yourself and treat yourself with kindness and respect, and care about yourself enough to want to keep on growing and evolving a little each day.

130. Your future is what you make it.

Every single choice you make shapes what happens next, which is exciting because it means that *you* are in control of your future and you can have, be and do absolutely anything you like. So, what will your future look like?

131. One step at a time.

You don't have to have all the answers right now... and in fact you never will, because there are so many variables in life that you'll never be able to work out what will or won't happen in the future. Instead of trying to get too far ahead of yourself, just focus on the current step and the next one. It makes life a lot less overwhelming!

132. Look up and reconnect with the wider world.

You are part of a much bigger world than what is just in front of you, and yet it can be easy to find ourselves distracted by our phones or our day-to-day lives so you need to regularly remind yourself to pay attention to the bigger stuff in order to not become isolated or narrow-focused. Make time to consciously look up and discover more of the world outside of just your immediate day-to-day existence, because that's how you grow.

133. Focus on one thing at a time.

You can try to do 18 different things at once, but I guarantee you that none of them will have your 100% effort and they won't be done as well as if you have completed them one at a time. Why? Because you're not a superhero, and that means you can't give your all to multiple things at once. When you focus on one thing at a time, and you give it your full and undivided attention, you can deliver a much better result… and one that is far more rewarding, because you put the effort in to create better quality.

134. Pause. Often.

We spend so much of our time rushing through life and thinking that we need to quickly react to things so that we can get on with the next task… but taking the time to pause every now and then allows your mind time to process things, and you'll then find you're much better equipped to handle challenges if you stop reacting and, instead, take the time to pause and *then* respond.

135. Even the roughest of seas can take you to wonderful new places.

Life is never going to be rainbows and unicorns 100% of the time, and yet even our most challenging times can serve a positive purpose if we choose to learn from them. I wouldn't be doing the work I do now, which I absolutely love, without having experienced some truly awful times in my past. You never know what is just over the horizon.

136. Be true to yourself.

There is nobody in this world exactly the same as you, and that is what makes you special, so don't try to be someone or something that you're not. It took me a long time to learn that just being myself and doing what I love felt *way* better than trying to make people like me whose opinion I didn't actually care about. Be you.

137. Sometimes you have to make tough choices.

There are things in life you can control and things you cannot. That means being prepared to make the tough choices if and when you need to. It might not always be the choice you want to make, but sometimes what you need is more important than what you want.

138. Find wonder in the little things.

Madonna was right when she sang that you don't need diamond rings or eighteen karat gold. It's the small things that matter most, like a friend's smile or that warm and fuzzy feeling you get when you cuddle your pet. Learn to appreciate the little things in life more often and you'll discover greater joy.

139. Reminder: you can walk away from toxic people and situations.

You may not have any control over what someone else says or does, but you most certainly have control over who has access to you. If something or someone is toxic, address the issue and then, if it continues, walk away. Your peace of mind is more important than anything else.

140. Something new is always just around the corner.

Today is just one day out of a whole bunch of days, and there is always something new to discover and experience. If you're having a tough time today, then remember that this day is only 24 hours long and tomorrow is a brand new day full of endless possibility.

141. Enjoy the journey.

I am an absolute dork about how much I love travelling by train, and I have been that way since I was a small child, and I think that the main reason for that is there's something about the journey itself that makes me feel inspired and excited. Life is a journey that's worthy of us getting excited about as well. Savour every moment of *every* journey you take, no matter how big or small.

142. From little things, big things can grow.

Every single tree once started out as a tiny seed or acorn, and every single product or piece of art in the world was once nothing more than a single idea in someone's mind. Plant seeds, water them and nurture them, and over time they will grow into something big and mighty.

143. Write your own story.

When it comes to your life, it's your life and nobody else's; you get to create your own narrative by making choices that feel aligned with who you are and what you value. If you're doing no harm, being kind and giving more than you take, then do what brings you joy.

144. Give yourself the gift of peace of mind.

It's so easy to get caught up in all of the things going on around us, and in the wider world, but the fact is that your peace of mind is more important than any other consideration because it gives you a solid foundation. When given a choice between drama and peace, choose peace of mind. I'd even tho so far as to say that you should go out of your way to create peace of mind in your life (it just so happens to be the number one item on my priority list, which then guides what I choose to do with my time).

145. What matters most is what you do today.

The only way to shape your future into whatever you want it to be is to stop stressing about tomorrow and instead start focusing on making the most of today, because what you do today creates tomorrow. Look after the present and the future will look after itself.

146. Growth requires letting go.

Old habits probably won't serve your best interests as you grow, and you may even find that some people in your life aren't on board with the way you're changing (which is about them, not you). Sometimes you have to let go of the old to make way for the new.

147. Being positive doesn't mean ignoring the negative.

There will always be challenging and difficult things going on around you, and in the world at large, and part of having a healthy mindset is being realistic about the good and not-so-good of life. A positive outlook involves accepting the negatives that are out of your control and choosing to counterbalance them with the positive, instead of allowing them to eat away at your soul. It's a matter of choice and a matter of focus.

148. Never change who you are to make others comfortable.

You can still be kind and respectful of others without having to reduce yourself into something that you're not. Find balance in all things.

149. Whatever you've been holding off on doing, just do it.

Send off that application, book that vacation, learn that new skill, write that book… do that thing you've been afraid of doing, because you'll never know if you never try. Small steps add up to big results.

150. Learn how to celebrate yourself.

It's wonderful when other people give us nice feedback and encouragement, but all too often we forget to be that cheerleader for ourselves. Self-love, self-compassion and self-worth all start with the word 'self' for a good reason.

151. Feel what you need to feel.

The thing with feelings is that you need to feel them, process them and let them go when you have learned what they are trying to teach you. If you try to fight them or resist them then you can make things worse for yourself, and if you let them control you then that creates challenges as well. See your feelings as clues rather than facts.

152. It's less about what you're attracting and more about what you're choosing.

There will always be challenging things going on, and difficult people to contend with. Rather than thinking that you're attracting them, instead remind yourself that you get to choose what stays and what goes in your life. It's the choices you make today that shape your tomorrow.

153. We won't agree all of the time, and that's OK.

You're not always going to like everything I say and do, and I'm not always going to like everything you say and do, because we are all unique individuals with our own viewpoint and it's impossible to agree 100% of the time. Know the difference between having a difference of opinion versus dealing with toxicity. I generally find the line is intention; if someone is clearly intending to be nasty or hateful towards others, then it's time to put a stop to the crap.

154. All things take time.

There's a reason why we have sayings like "Rome wasn't built in a day" — have you seen Rome? It's massive! All things take time, effort and perseverance, so that means that not only do you need to consistently show up and do the work but you also need to choose to be patient and determined. Results very rarely happen overnight, and even if they do they are rarely sustainable in the long term. Keep going.

155. Life is trial and error.

If you want to grow and evolve then you have to try new things, and if it doesn't work then that's OK; just try something else. It's better to try and fail than never know, and it's OK to change your mind; I did it a while ago with TikTok and I very quickly realised it's not for me (it's a bit like the Wild West), but I'm glad I tried it rather than wondering "what if?". Mistakes and failures are an important part of how we learn and how we grow.

156. Most of your worries will never eventuate.

Whatever you're currently worried about, you're probably overthinking it and I'm going to guess that you won't remember it in five months, let alone five years. Worry is wasted energy because it robs us of our peace of mind today. Write your worries down and look for potential solutions that are within your direct control. And if it's out of your control? Well then it's out of your control, so let it go. What will be will be.

157. What has happened has happened.

When we deal with tough situations, or things that hurt us, often we spend ages going over and over the thing… but that serves little purpose other than to keep us stuck in the emotion of it. Can you change it? No, because what's done is done. Can you learn from it and grow? Yes, absolutely! But you can only do that once you make your peace with the fact that no amount of revisiting it will change what did or didn't happen because it is what it is. Accept it and move forward by learning the lesson.

158. Change is essential.

Look, I know change can be painful and I know that sometimes we might want things to stay the way they are, but change is a natural part of life and it's necessary. Think of it this way: everything ages and decays, and so change is the process that keeps everything moving forward instead of just letting it all rot around us. Nothing lasts forever and that's OK; it's the fleeting nature of life that makes it so beautiful. Change might be painful, but it brings with it renewal and hope.

159. Make your emotional health a priority.

With so much going on throughout the world for the last few years, it's easy to get caught up in a tidal wave of feelings and emotions… but all you can control is what is within your direct control: you, and what you choose to say and do. Start with a foundation of managing your emotional health through plenty of rest, taking time for yourself, and expressing your emotions in a healthy way through journaling or therapy (or both). If you feel drained, take a step back and devote some time to yourself… and remember to take things one day at a time. You will be OK.

160. Healing is a journey, not a destination.

You don't wake up one day and discover that you've magically healed from your difficulties and traumas; it's a lifelong process of learning how to live with it and healing a little each day. So don't wait until you've healed to live your life because then you'll miss out on the very thing that helps you to heal, which is choosing to live life to the fullest in spite of everything you've experienced in the past.

161. There's a big difference between 'moving on' and 'moving forward'.

When you move on it often involves trying to forget about whatever happened or didn't happen, whereas moving forward means first taking the time to reflect on it so you can learn what you need to learn in order to grow. Even difficult and challenging times have something to teach us and everything we experience changes us in some way, big or small. Your growth is found in taking time to honour all of your experiences so that you can make your peace with them and then move forward.

162. Do nothing.

Sometimes your brain just needs a bit of a rest, so that it can take the time it needs to recharge (and that actually helps you to function better because it can improve your cognitive processing). So, stop trying to fill every second of every day and let yourself have a few minutes here and there of doing nothing; look out the window, sit outside and stare at the sky, close your eyes and be quietly mindful. Your brain will thank you for it.

163. Less focus on 'what if?' and more focus on what is.

When you spend your time thinking about what could have been or what should have been, you're taking your eyes off what truly matters: *what is*. You cannot change what has or hasn't happened in the past, but you can definitely change what happens next by means of your words and actions. That's how you create a life for yourself that feels meaningful, fulfilling and satisfying.

164. Make thoughtful choices.

There are plenty of things you could choose to do with your time on Earth, but let's be really honest here: not all of them are healthy, and some of them are downright stupid. If you want to have a life that feels satisfying and meaningful, then you need to make thoughtful and considered choices. That doesn't mean that you can't have fun, but it does mean you need to think about what matters most to you and look after yourself.

165. You don't need to have all the answers right now.

Most of us are really just making things up as we go along (actually, I think all of us are… but some people aren't willing to admit that!), so the thing is that if you wait until you feel like everything is perfect then you'll be waiting for eternity. Sometimes you just need to take that first step and be willing to learn along the way. Just focus on doing your best today and trust that tomorrow will be OK.

166. Know the difference between opinion and fact.

Opinions are like podcasts; it seems like everyone's got one, and most of them are full of noise. Just because you don't like a fact, that doesn't make it untrue; sometimes we have to accept that and then make our peace with the things that are outside of our control. And, while we're at it, please remember to never let someone's opinion hold you back from being true to yourself.

167. No dream is too big to turn into reality.

You can have, be and do basically anything that you want to with enough time, effort and perseverance; it requires you to do the work, build the skills, and be patient. And if it becomes challenging, remember what Billy Ocean told us in the 1980's: When The Going Gets Tough, The Tough Get Going.

168. Treat others how you want to be treated.

Have you ever heard that old expression "two wrongs don't make a right"? It's a way of saying that if you get into a disagreement with someone, don't try to fight fire with fire; not only will you just get a bigger fire, you'll also create a much bigger conflict by just immediately arguing back with them. Arguments rarely lead to constructive solutions, so be calm and fair in order to de-escalate the situation. And, generally speaking, don't be nasty to people… if for no other reason than what you put out comes back to you.

169. Healing takes work.

Time does not heal all wounds; doing the work does. When we work through our feelings about the experiences we've had in our lives in a constructive and objective way, we begin to take away the power those experiences hold over us. Doing that takes courage and also, ideally, support from a professional or the people who care about you (or, better yet, from both).

170. Some advice is just toxic.

Do you know what I absolutely hate? When you see advice from people that basically suggests you're at fault for your own trauma and suffering because you didn't think positively enough. You're not. I know firsthand how challenging and difficult it is to work through traumatic experiences. However what I *will* say is that the choice to confront it and work through it is always yours; not doing anything might seem safer, but nothing changes if nothing changes. But do feel free to tell the Toxic Positivity™ people to shut the hell up while you're doing so!

171. There is no magic formula to life.

We seem to think that we have to follow a very specific path in order to earn the right to be seen as successful… but that's just not true. You don't have to earn your place in this world. You don't have to achieve a specific set of goals or pass Level 18 in order to be considered a 'worthy' human being. I consider true success to be living a life that feels meaningful to you, and what that looks and feels like is nobody's business but yours. Do no harm, be kind and give more than you take, and to hell with what others think about you!

172. Consistency is what creates lasting change.

The boring fact of life is that all things take time, effort and perseverance; overnight success is incredibly rare and even if it does happen, it's no guarantee of lasting success or achievement. Know what you want to achieve and why, do the work, and be flexible so you can adapt and respond to changing circumstances. One day at a time, one step at a time!

173. You deserve to be appreciated.

Every single person on this planet deserves to be acknowledged, valued and respected… so if that's not happening in any of your relationships, demand better. And if you don't get it, move on. You are worthy of kindness and love, so never settle for anything less than fairness and respect.

174. What you do next is your choice.

Life is a series of choices, and each decision you make takes you down a new path. That might sound a bit overwhelming, especially if you're dealing with worry or indecisiveness, but it's actually an amazing opportunity to create your own life in a way that feels honest and authentic for you. Make choices that balance both your head and your heart, and that are grounded in kindness (to others and to yourself), and you'll be OK.

175. Own who you are.

In a world where you can be anything and anyone you want, why would you choose to be anything other than your true self? If you do no harm, are kind and give more than you take, then it really doesn't matter what other people think; be 100% yourself without apology, because it is your uniqueness that makes you so invaluable to this world… so, own it.

176. All things take practice.

Very few people pick up a paintbrush for the first time and create a masterpiece; hardly anyone can just sit down at a piano and begin to play beautifully. Skills are developed over time, so even if you're not good at something today that doesn't mean you can't be great at it in the future with enough time, effort and perseverance. Take small steps every day and keep going.

177. Tomorrow is a new day.

If you're ever having a rough day, remember that tomorrow really is a new day and you never know what is just around the corner, so keep going. Even if tomorrow were just a tiny fraction better than today, and the day after were just a tiny bit better than that, over time that all adds up to be so much better than where things are today. That's how I managed to get through the worst of my own battle with depression and anxiety a few years back, and I can tell you that it does eventually get better. You *will* be OK.

178. Don't settle.

Sometimes we might think that we have to 'just make do' or that 'fine' is good enough… do you know what 'fine' is? That's future boredom waiting to happen. I don't think everything in life needs to be fireworks and excitement, and I think that satisfaction is more important than happiness, but if you just feel 'meh' about something? That's settling, and settling does not lead to satisfaction in the long term. You deserve true satisfaction.

179. Don't act in anger.

Sometimes you're going to feel frustrated, annoyed, pissed off, furious, enraged or angry… but when you make decisions based on those emotions, you usually wind up making a mess that will take a lot more than a mop and bucket to clean up. Feel what you need to feel but rather than just reacting instead choose to pause and give time for your emotions to settle, before you then use your rational mind to think about how to respond thoughtfully. It will make life *much* better for your future self.

180. Real peace of mind comes from within.

Do you know why I regularly point out that there's no magic pill you can take to fix everything? Because there's not. Nothing and nobody can create peace of mind for you; it's up to you to do the work. Medication can help and it plays a necessary role in many cases, but it isn't the be-all and end-all for managing mental health conditions. I know how tiring that can seem, and if you're finding it difficult to deal with things then you really should get support from a professional (like a counsellor or therapist), but always remember that true peace comes from within, so stop expecting to find it elsewhere.

181. Open your own doors.

Create your own opportunities in life instead of hoping that they will just come to you, because they probably won't. That's how I started my podcast in late 2019 and it's led me to places I never would have imagined. And while we're on the subject, know that not everything you try will work and that's OK; a failure is only a failure if it doesn't teach you something. Just keep on opening those doors for yourself.

182. Tap in to your creativity.

We spend so much of our lives penned in by social norms and other peoples' expectations that we forget we can have, be and do absolutely anything we want to, with enough time, effort and perseverance. Forget about trying to 'think outside the box' — get rid of that box entirely and use your creativity to take you to amazing new places.

183. Today is the day.

It doesn't matter what you've done or haven't done in the past; each new day is an opportunity to shape your life into something new. You cannot change the past, you can only learn from it… so how are you going to take everything you've experienced — the good, the bad and everything in between — and use it to begin making choices that create a better tomorrow for yourself? This really is the beginning of the rest of your life.

184. Nobody can 'make' you happy.

It's a total cliché to say this but I'll say it anyway: happiness is an inside job. External things and other people can certainly contribute towards your happiness, but to actually feel happy and satisfied requires you to go within and allow yourself to truly experience happiness. Other people can support you and contribute to you creating that feeling, but they cannot do it for you and they cannot be the source of that happiness… only you can do that. So, look within and work on whatever is holding you back from true happiness and satisfaction.

185. Truth can never be silenced.

No matter how hard some people might try to push their own agendas, the truth can never and will never be silenced. Sometimes it might feel like we're living in the Wild, Wild West of history, where anything goes, but I promise you that if you stay the course and continue to speak up and speak out, the truth can never remain hidden for long. All things take time, effort and perseverance. And, by the way, please don't automatically believe everything you read on social media; ask questions and approach things with a critical eye.

186. Life is simpler than we make it.

Sometimes people seem genuinely surprised when I say that life is better when you choose to do no harm, be kind, and give more than you take; I mean, it was hardly going to be to do more harm, be a dick, and take, take, take, was it… unless you're trying to be a politician. Anyway, my point is that we tend to overcomplicate things a lot; my general philosophy is to keep things as simple as possible and to make your peace of mind your number one priority. Oh, and don't be a dick… that's always a good one to remember!

187. Search within.

Look within yourself for the things you are seeking, instead of trying to find them externally. You're not going to find your self worth in someone else or in 'things' or job titles or whatever, because when all of those things are stripped away, all you are left with is yourself… and so that is where your search must begin and end. Explore who you really are and what brings you joy, and discover how to make a life for yourself that feels purposeful and meaningful.

188. Closure is something you give yourself.

I know first-hand how much it can feel like we need to have all of our questions answered or wanting to be able to say our piece when someone has hurt us or wronged us, but frankly it rarely ever works out the way we imagine it; you'll usually be left with more questions than answers. Sometimes the only closure you need is to recognise that you deserve better and that you, and only you, are responsible for your own peace of mind. Let go.

189. Leave people be.

Call me old fashioned but I enjoy the simple pleasures in life: a nice sunset, a good coffee, not sticking my nose into other peoples' business… you know, the basics. The older I get, the less I understand the desire to get involved in what other people are or are not doing. Does it impact me directly? Does it hurt me or others? If the answers to those questions are 'no' then I say you do you, boo boo, and I'll be over here minding my own business… because, really, who has the time and energy for drama? Not me!

190. Slow it down.

You don't have to achieve everything immediately and by consciously choosing to take your time with things, you allow yourself space to explore ideas and discover new things. And if you ever find yourself feeling like you need to rush, just remember what those wise philosophers the Spice Girls said: "Hey you always on the run, gotta slow it down baby, gotta have some fun."

191. Healing takes time.

When we experience loss it can feel like you might never laugh again, love again, experience joy again… but you will. Grief doesn't just magically disappear one day; you simply learn how to integrate the loss into your life. At first it's like a sharp and pointy kind of pain, and over time the edges get worn down and become dull; the pain is still there, but it's less painful and you can begin to live with it. You will be OK. Grief is the price of love.

192. You don't have to prove yourself to anyone.

When I was a teenager I had a lot of trouble fitting in anywhere (and a lot of that stemmed back to rejection issues from my childhood after my father left, but that's a discussion for another day). It took me a very long time to learn the two most important lessons in life: if people like you for you, great! And if they don't like you for you, also great! Wait, *what*?! Look, I know rejection feels horrible when it's happening but I can tell you with absolute certainty that it's a good thing because it serves to remove those people from your life. Surround yourself with 'your' people and you will flourish!

193. Choose the company you keep.

The people around us have a strong influence on how we behave, and so you need to think about the choices you make. If someone brings out the worst in you or you find yourself saying and doing things that aren't in line with the type of person you want to be, then you need to distance yourself from them. You can't change the people around you, but you can change the people around you.

194. Nothing takes the past away like the future.

I can't take the credit for this one; it's a line from my favourite Madonna song *Nothing Really Matters* from the late 90's and I've shared it many times in my podcast because it's true… each day is a fresh start and you can choose to create whatever new future you want for yourself. We are never stuck in the past unless we choose to allow ourselves to be stuck. Create your own future.

195. Other peoples' feelings are not your responsibility.

All-too-often we can find ourselves hiding who we are and denying our own needs in order to 'keep the peace' with the people we're closest to, but that causes you pain and suffering. Be kind and respectful of others, but don't deny who you are. You cannot control how others feel and you need to be true to yourself. Remember: we are all in control of how we choose to behave, so you are not responsible for what others do or don't do.

196. Most of what you think you know is wrong.

Look, I don't want to rattle your cage or shake your belief systems to the core (or maybe I do?!) but, to be frank, most of what we hold to be true is actually just a series of collective beliefs that we've all agreed to over the last few hundred years or more. Work looks the way it looks because that's what we've always done. Money has value only because we say it does. Life is about far more than just going through the motions every day and following everyone else. Ask questions and create a life for yourself that feels truly meaningful and satisfying.

197. Take regular time off.

You know how you get a certain number of vacation days every year? Use them every year! Without adequate time off, all you're doing is pushing yourself to work, work, work… you need time to rest, recover and recharge and that means having time for yourself. And, on that note, do not answer work calls or emails on your time off under any circumstances! You're entitled to a regular break so take an actual break. You'll feel better for it.

198. Wisdom is true wealth.

The only true power is gaining wisdom; the wisdom to do better and be better one small step at a time. How much money you have or what power you have is irrelevant; those things only have value because we think they do, but they're pointless. The more you learn about life the more you realise how much there is to learn, and when you gain the wisdom to see the world with humility and wonder you gain the ability to find true satisfaction in life.

199. What you say and do matters more than the how.

It's now easier than ever before to share your message with others around the world and so instead of trying to compete with others by creating Hollywood-level videos or wanting to create the next million-download podcast, instead focus on the quality of the message you're sharing and remember that simple is best.

200. Trends change, truth is eternal.

Have you ever watched something from 10, 20, 30 years ago and cringed at how tacky it seems now? And then have you ever seen something or heard something from the past and gone, "wow, that aged well!"? The difference is that stuff that follows trends will always age badly, whereas focusing on quality and authenticity is timeless. That's why trends change so fast on social media, because we get bored of them quickly. Just be yourself and don't feel you have to chase what everyone else is doing.

201. Your feelings aren't permanent.

Nothing lasts forever, not even those challenging or upsetting feelings you might be having. When you remind yourself of this fundamental fact of life, you can begin to learn how to make your peace with the tough times because you know that behind every cloud the sun is waiting to shine again. You will be OK.

202. Be someone who inspires you.

Often we look to others as examples of who and what we think we should be or could be, and I think that's fine if we do that in a healthy and objective way but the goal should ideally be to inspire yourself. How do you do that? Well, you start by choosing to celebrate your strengths and then taking small steps every day to work on the aspects of yourself you want to improve. Create a life for yourself that inspires you to get out of bed each morning, and be someone you feel proud to be, and you'll find greater satisfaction in life.

203. It's never too late to change course.

You can choose to head in a new direction at any time, regardless of your age or circumstances; it may not always be easy, but it's definitely possible. I went back to school in my late 30's to study psychology and sociology, and although it was *very* challenging and I was twice the age of most of the other students, I was able to take my career — and my life — in a totally new direction. You're in control of what you choose to do with your life, at whatever age.

204. Let go of the past to make way for the future.

When you let your past take up space in your head rent-free, you make it hard to see all of the possibilities in front of you today… and it's by taking those possibilities and turning them into reality that you create your own future. There's a reason why our heads only allow us to look one direction at a time: you can't look forward if you're still looking back. Process what you need to, make your peace with it, and let go so you can keep moving forward.

205. Sometimes you need a mental health day.

If you're feeling a bit low then it can help to give yourself a break for a few hours or even a day or two. That means giving yourself time to rest and replenish without trying to cram 50 different things into your time and without feeling guilty for giving yourself a break. It's OK to take time off if and when you need it, and sometimes just giving yourself permission to take a break and do nothing other than looking after your mental health can be exactly what you need to release those crappy feelings.

206. Listen to what you need.

There's a big difference between our wants and our needs; our wants are our desires and we can survive without them, whereas our needs are… well, they're what we need! I talked about this in Episode 137 of my podcast, but basically I suggest you think of it this way: if you need a break, take it. If you need space, take it. If you need time to think about something, take it. If you need to prioritise your wellbeing, do it (and that one should be a given anyway, because nobody's going to do it for you!). Don't feel guilty for doing what you need to do.

207. Stop trying to please your inner critic.

Actually, stop trying to please critics in general, because you never will, but that rings especially true when it comes to that critical voice in your head that's determined to make you feel bad about anything and everything — it's never going to be satisfied, so don't try. Instead, learn to remind yourself that your thoughts are not facts and focus your energy on doing things you feel proud of.

208. Things don't get better. You do.

We seem to really like saying that things can only get better (hey, someone even wrote a song about it back in the 90's…) but that focuses on the external, which you have no control over; you can only control yourself and what you do and say, and so things get better because we slowly learn how to live with them and how to make our peace with the things that have hurt us or that we find challenging. If you're struggling today then know this: things really do get better when you learn how to lean into your own strength by changing what you can control, and accepting the things you can't control.

209. Stop rushing.

When you go about your day at a frantic pace, you're not allowing yourself time to savour the small moments — and those are the ones where you're most likely to find greater satisfaction. I talked about this in Episode 140 of my podcast and I highly recommend you make time each day to slow down and enjoy the moment; even just five minutes a day will make an enormous difference to the way you feel about life.

210. Your work is not your identity.

How many times have you met someone new and the first thing that comes out of their mouth is, "what do you do for a living"? We're socially conditioned to attached our identity to what we do for work but your job doesn't define you; your job is what you do, not who you are. Take the time to really get to know yourself and be clear on who you are (and who you are not) outside of your work, because that's the real version of you. We all have to do what we have to do to earn a living, but nobody ever said it had to become our entire identity.

211. Be present.

When you give all or most of your attention to the past or the future, you miss out on the present moment — and this is where life is actually lived. The past has passed and the future is unknown, and so it's really only this moment we have for certain; being fully present helps us find greater satisfaction and a sense of calm (and I talked about how to be present in Episode 83 of my podcast). As the writer Eckhart Tolle once said, "Stress is caused by being 'here' but wanting to be 'there'".

212. Be the kind of person you admire.

I have a bit of an issue with the whole 'celebrity culture' thing that's so common in society because I think that instead of focusing so much on what others are doing we should be turning our attention to what we do as individuals and, more importantly, how we do it. People are just people and nobody is perfect, so when you buy in to the whole 'cult of personality' thing that goes with admiring certain people, you're setting yourself up for disappointment. Instead of admiring others, be someone that you admire.

213. If you want to improve your life, improve your life.

You are in full control of what you do and do not do with your life, so if you want things to be better then you have to do the work to make them better… and that's something that you, and only you, can do. If you want to grow then it's up to you to grow. Learn new skills, explore your interests, discover new ideas, remove negative relationships and build more positive relationships, let go of unhealthy habits, beliefs and behaviours, seek support if you're struggling with aspects of your wellbeing. Growth doesn't come because you want it to happen; growth comes because you make it happen.

214. Nobody knows you like you.

Nobody on this planet will ever be able to know you 100% because we are all complex and unique individuals, and so that means that it's important for you to really take the time to get to know yourself in order to be the most authentic version of yourself possible. You get to choose what people see or don't see of you and how much they know of who you really are; choose to let people in so they can connect with the real you.

215. Think before you speak.

Before you say something to or about another person, stop and think. Is it harmful or is it kind? Is it negative, or is it positive? Is it really the type of energy you want to put out into the world? Our words and actions have consequences, so choose to do no harm, be kind and give more than you take… because what you put out comes back to you. Each of us can create a kinder world one step at a time, one thoughtful action at a time.

216. People are people.

Aside from being a classic 80's song by Depeche Mode, 'people are people' serves as a simple reminder that we are ALL human; instead of fighting one another, we should be choosing to show one another kindness... and that's a choice you can make every day, in every interaction you have. It doesn't matter what someone's skin colour, heritage, gender, religion or sexuality is... we're all the same on the inside, so treat everyone the same. In other words, don't be a dick to people!

217. Be open to learning.

Someone once said to me that the same types of lessons will appear over and over again until you eventually learn what you need to learn, and that's definitely a pattern I've seen in my own life. Whether it's the types of relationships you have and the people you encounter, or if it's more to do with particular aspects of yourself that keep on showing up, there are many different lessons we need to learn in life; if you resist them, they tend to just keep on popping up time and time again. Learn what you need to learn, even if those lessons are tough.

218. If you don't know what you want, start with what you don't want.

Sometimes it can be hard to work out what it is that we really want or need, and when that happens I find it helps to begin by identifying what you absolutely don't want; that usually comes to you a lot more easily and then it can help you to begin to think about what you *do* want instead. For example, I know I don't want to work for someone else again and I also don't want to ever wear a tie again, so that thought process helped me to start thinking about how I might potentially be able to work for myself instead (and now that's what I do). Everything has something to teach you, including the stuff you don't like.

219. Don't just exist. Live.

It wasn't until well after my breakdown in late 2011/throughout 2012 that I realised I had been just going through the motions in my life and that I was trying to find purpose and meaning through all the external things that we're taught to value from a young age like job title, money, status and what other people think of us. But all of those things don't help you to actually like who you are as a person, and that's the difference between existing versus actually living; when you can take responsibility for your own life and find genuine satisfaction in who you are, that's when you begin to truly live.

220. Not everyone will respect your boundaries.

There's a curious thing that happens when you begin to set and maintain healthy boundaries for yourself: some people will be respectful, and others will react in an immature and selfish way… and, funnily enough, that serves to demonstrate *exactly* why you need boundaries with them. They might create drama with you or block you or just generally act out, but understand that their reaction says much more about them than it does you. Set clear, kind and healthy boundaries and stick to them.

221. Forgive yourself.

You know those things you've been carrying around for years that make you feel bad about yourself? Those grudges you hold towards your past self, those feelings you have about choices you made long ago? *Let it go*. Holding on to anger, hurt, sadness and regret just keeps you stuck in those feelings and it serves no useful purpose; all it does is serve to help you keep on punishing yourself over and over again. Learn what you need to learn from whatever happened or didn't happen, accept that you did the best you could at the time (even if you know you would do things differently now), and forgive yourself so you can let go. You can't move forward when you're stuck in the past.

222. Your choices create your life.

There will always be things going on around you — like the way other people behave, and world events — but the one thing you always have control over is you and, more specifically, your own choices. What you choose to do and say (or not do or say) shapes what happens next. So, if you're not happy with the way things are in your life then it's up to you — and only you — to make choices that create the type of life you *do* want.

223. Reconnect with your soul.

Most of the things we fill our lives with bear no actual connection to the essence of who we truly are. Our humanity is defined by our ability to connect, to create, to learn, to grow and, most importantly, to love. If you feel out of alignment, begin by considering how you can reconnect with the stuff that truly matters and let go of everything else. You don't have to become a monk or give away all your possessions to live a life that feels like you're truly living, instead of just going through the motions. Live by connecting with the essence of who you really are.

224. Boxes are for parcels, not people.

When you try to fit into a box, you wind up disregarding all the other unique aspects of who you are as a person. Diversity is what makes life interesting; how boring would this world be if we were all the same?! Instead of trying to force yourself into the boxes that society creates for you or that you think you have to be in, instead choose to be yourself and forge your own path. It's certainly a lot more fun.

225. Less excuses, more solutions.

When we make excuses for things or when we try to find someone to blame, all we do is waste time and energy that could be used to find practical solutions to our issues and challenges. No amount of finger-pointing or excuse-making will ever change the reality of a situation, so focus on the way forward rather than what is behind you. Whether you look for problems or you look for solutions, what you seek is what you will find.

226. Small changes have big results.

We often think we need to completely change our lives or make massive, sweeping changes in order to grow, but really it's much simpler than that. Pick a few things you want to work on or achieve, break them down into their smallest possible steps, and do a little each day. Yes, it requires time, effort and perseverance (not to mention patience), but when you change things gradually it tends to be much more sustainable in the long-term because it's easier to stick with it. Small steps lead to big results.

227. Looks fade. Kind is forever.

There's an old saying that 'beauty is only skin deep' and if you think about it, there are plenty of people who might look attractive on the outside but have dark and ugly souls. When you focus on what's inside, the outside will take care of itself; sure, you might never win a beauty pageant, but does that *really* matter? When you choose to be kind to others and to yourself, it fills you with an inner joy and greater confidence (plus other peoples' crap tends to affect you much less). Be kind.

228. Only you can decide what you do.

There's a saying by the ancient philosopher Socrates that goes, "I cannot teach anybody anything. I can only make them think." That's one of my favourites because it reminds us all that we are in full control over what we do or do not do with our lives, and it means that the responsibility for changing, evolving and growing sits firmly and solely with each of us as individuals. You can choose to grow or you can choose to stay stuck; choose wisely.

229. In any argument, think before you speak.

Do you know what happens when you try to fight fire with fire? You end up with a bigger fire. The surest way to make an argument escalate into a full-blown conflict is to react without thinking, because then we're operating on pure emotions and our emotions don't consider the big picture. Pause, count to ten, and then let your logical mind catch up with your feelings so you can respond in a more thoughtful, considered and balanced way.

230. It takes time to adapt to grief.

Grief doesn't stop, you just learn how to live with it. When we experience a deep loss, it's like there's a part of us that is missing and we need to adapt to that loss… which is painful. I once heard grief described as being 'love with nowhere to go' and I think that's a great description; it doesn't just disappear over time, because grief is something that continues and what actually changes is you as you learn how to adapt to it and live with it. The pain remains, but it's less sharp and painful over time.

231. Find the right balance for you.

I'm a firm believer that life satisfaction is all about having a healthy balance and a sense of moderation in all things, and you have to find what that balance is for you. For me it's cultivating a sense of calm and peace of mind while also not putting up with crap, which I do by setting and maintaining healthy boundaries and also focusing on what really matters to me (so I can let go of the stuff that doesn't matter). What about you?

232. Challenge yourself.

When you play safe you might stay safe, but nothing changes if nothing changes. The choices that seem scary and uncomfortable are usually the ones with the most to teach us, because they push us out of our comfort zone and challenge us to grow. Ships aren't built to stay safe in the harbour.

233. Learn to enjoy your own company.

I love spending time with the people I care about, but I also really love spending time on my own because it's when I get to think about things more deeply and it plays an enormous role in my creativity. There is true strength to be found in learning how to be OK with being alone; remember, there's an enormous difference between being lonely and being alone. Find a healthy balance between time with others and time with yourself.

234. Maturity takes work.

When you choose to be proactive about learning and growing as a human being, that's maturity. When you choose to remain stuck in old patterns of thinking that are harmful and unkind, that's immaturity. If the point of life is to grow and be the best version of yourself possible (which I truly believe it is), then why would you choose to remain small when you can choose to grow and evolve? It takes work, but the work is definitely worth it for finding satisfaction and meaning in your life.

235. Your feelings do not define you.

Look, we all have thoughts and feelings sometimes that we wouldn't exactly describe as 'positive', but they don't define you; it's what you choose to do with negative thoughts and feelings that matters most. Do you choose to latch on to them and let them drag you down into a spiral of negativity, or do you choose to just observe them and let them pass you by? Your thoughts and feelings are not facts, and it's what you choose to do with them that defines you. Choose thoughtfully.

236. Compassion beats judgement.

When people judge others they're saying, "I'm so insecure that I have to project all of my negative thoughts onto others just to feel validated." Seriously, what's up with that? I don't know about you, but I have *much* better things to do with my time and energy… and, frankly, I don't care how you live your life provided it isn't harming anyone (which is why I like to call out bigoted and judgemental behaviour, because that is doing harm). Choose compassion. It's the kindest choice.

237. Never let somebody else determine your worth.

What others think about you is their issue, not yours; never, ever let someone demean you or make you feel less-than, and certainly never allow someone else to take advantage of you. Choose the people around you wisely and be proactive about removing negative influences from your life, because you deserve so much better. That involves knowing your worth and celebrating what makes you unique (and I explored how to improve your self worth in Episode 78 of my podcast, *Let's Talk About Mental Health*).

238. Stop waiting for tomorrow.

Many of us are guilty of waiting for things to 'eventually' get better or even just wishing that our day or week would hurry up and finish… when you do that you miss out on the present, which is the only place that life actually exists. Don't wish away today for a tomorrow that may never come; life will always have its ups and downs, so the challenge is to learn how to be satisfied here in this moment.

239. Don't let other people bring you down.

You know how sometimes other people might treat you like crap or be nasty to you for no obvious reason? That is 100% on them and it's not about you. I mean, surely we all understand that being a dick to other people and tearing them to pieces isn't a healthy thing to do… right?! So don't let that poor behaviour make you feel bad about yourself; they're the one with something wrong, not you! Choose to do no harm, be kind and give more than you take, and steer clear of morons.

240. Letting go might take many attempts.

I recently found myself getting frustrated when an old insecurity reared its ugly head in my mind, because I thought I had managed to let it go, but the reality of life is that it can take us a few times (or more) to make our peace with things — especially the stuff that's deep down in our core. That doesn't make you a failure; it makes you human. And think of it this way: each time you work on letting go of something, you chip a bit of it away… and so eventually it will no longer have power over you. Keep going.

241. Be real.

In a world where fakeness and insincerity seem to be completely fine, and even aspirational (I'm looking at you, social media), the most outrageously inspiring thing you can do is to be completely, absolutely, 100% yourself. When we try to be something that we're not, we end up missing out on the whole point of life: to be the best version of yourself possible. Don't try to change yourself to fit in; be yourself and you'll find where you fit in. You'll also feel a hell of a lot more satisfied with your life because you're being true to yourself!

242. Celebrate how far you've come.

We spend a huge amount of time focused on the next thing and the next thing after that… but what about all the progress you've made to reach this point, here and now? There was once a version of you who dreamt of this, so honour your progress. I think it's often human nature to default to future-based thinking, but you can consciously choose to pause and return to the present at any time (since this moment is where life is actually lived).

243. Struggles are not failures.

Why do we beat ourselves up for having challenges and difficult times? I'll tell you why: because we've been socially conditioned since childhood that we must always be getting better and putting our best foot forward, so struggling feels like a step backwards. It's not. Having difficult times in life is completely natural (I mean, life is a hot mess sometimes) and recognising you're struggling is actually the beginning of the process of healing. Take things one day at a time, do the work and get support if you need it.

244. Celebrate kindness, not bank balances.

If I see one more article or social media post celebrating someone just because they're a billionaire, I think I might be sick. Look, money is important in terms of making sure you have security and basic comfort but why are we celebrating the acquisition of staggering amounts of wealth and treating these people like celebrities for no real reason other than their bank balances? How did we end up in this messed-up world?! I'm far more interested in who you are than what you have. Show me your riches of kindness.

245. Keep going.

There will be days when it feels like too much. Keep going. There will be days when you feel exhausted. Keep going. There will be days when it feels like things will never get better. Keep going, because they can get better and they *will* get better. Perseverance is the foundation of all things, because without it we would never make any progress. You didn't come this far to only come this far.

246. You can change your life.

This advice is less 'advice' and more of a wish for you from me: if there is some aspect of your life that leaves you feeling unsettled, unsatisfied or unfulfilled, I hope you know that you can change it for the better… because you can. I've done it many, many times and it certainly wasn't easy (and it was definitely more terrifying than riding a rollercoaster immediately after a big lunch) but it's both necessary and worth it. Life is made for living, not just existing.

247. Buy less, live more.

Now, I'm no minimalist and I like my stuff as much as the next person, but we need to remember that every single purchase we make comes with a set of consequences in terms of what we need to do to pay for it; the more you buy, the more you need to work and the more complicated life becomes. Next time you go to buy something, take a moment to think about the bigger picture of your life and decide if the cost (as in, the actual cost *and* the cost to your time, energy and emotions) is really worth it for whatever it is. When you spend more thoughtfully, you make more time to live thoughtfully.

248. Don't punish yourself for the past.

Have you made monumental mistakes in the past? Join the rest of us, myself included! The problem is that when you beat yourself up over things that you did or didn't do in the past, you do two things: first, you waste a whole bunch of energy because the past has passed and it can never be changed (no matter how many times you go over it), and second, you chip away at your sense of self worth… and that's a terrible way to live. Learn what you need to learn, forgive yourself, and move forward with a commitment to apply what you have learned.

249. You can let go.

Sometimes it feels so hard to let go of people and situations from our past because we might be trying to figure out what went wrong, or we might be holding out hope that things can be repaired. But the question you have to ask yourself is this: why are you trying to hold on to people and situations that have already let you go? I know, it hurts… but the past is the past and it cannot be changed. Give yourself the gift of peace of mind and let go. Your future self will thank you for it.

250. You deserve better.

You know those relationships and situations in your life that make you doubt yourself or, worse yet, feel bad about yourself? You deserve so much better. Never settle for something or someone that makes you feel less-than or that takes you away from living a life that feels meaningful and satisfying. A joyful life is not just a gift for the lucky few; it's available to every single one of us with time, effort and perseverance. You really do deserve better.

251. Don't focus on what you can't do. Focus on what you can.

Instead of focusing on what you can't do, choose instead to turn your focus to what you *can* do. Why? Well, it's because belief is a funny old thing and what you believe usually ends up creating your reality. If you believe you can't do something, then guess what? You won't be able to do it… and so your lack of self-belief becomes a self-fulfilling prophecy. When you turn your attention from problems to solutions, you find more and more that you can do. I talked about self belief in Episode 125 of my podcast if you'd like to find out more about how to manage your self belief in a healthy way.

252. Use your anger for positivity.

Never let your anger control you, because that's when it causes chaos, pain and suffering. Instead of letting it own you, you can choose to own it. Use your anger as fuel to shake things up and make changes that you might never have found the strength to make otherwise. Stand firm and tall, and use those emotions to drive you towards something far more positive and constructive than just pure anger — in other words, use your anger to create a better tomorrow.

253. What you do as a consenting adult is your business, and nobody else's.

Far too many people spend far too much time sticking their noses into other peoples' business. Just because you don't like something that doesn't make it wrong; it just makes it different. And sitting in judgment of others doesn't make you better; it just makes you unkind. Focus on doing no harm, being kind and giving more than you take, and don't worry about what narrow-minded people have to say.

254. Celebrate your progress.

Remember when you wanted what you have now? So then why aren't you celebrating where you are, instead of constantly focusing on the next thing and wanting more, more, more?! A huge part of learning how to really live your life to the fullest involves being able to see just how far you've come and making the most of this moment, here and now… because this is where life is lived, not in some future that may or may not happen. Be proud of where you are now and how far you've come.

255. Consciously create moments of calm for yourself daily.

Trying to cram too much into your day and running around like a cat with a case of the zoomies is not going to do anything other than wear you out, which is going to make it harder for you to feel satisfied in life. When you consciously make space for calm every single day, you lay the foundation for greater peace of mind and life satisfaction. Oh, and you won't look so frazzled all the time… so that's a plus!

256. Follow your dreams.

If you've always wanted to do something, do it. If you've always wanted to try something new, give it a go. Your life is yours to live, and so if you feel drawn to something then you may as well try to make your dreams and aspirations come true. Even if you fail or if things don't work out the way you had hoped, it's OK; it's the journey that matters more than the destination, and it's better to try and fail instead of spending the rest of your life wondering "what if?". And remember that the things you feel drawn to and passionate about are calling you for a reason, so don't ignore them.

257. There's no filter for real life.

Is it just me or do you also find the overly-processed, highly-perfectionist images of peoples' supposed lives on social media to be the most dull and boring thing ever? Life is messy and complicated, and when we only present a highlight reel of our best bits to the world we send a message to others — and to ourselves — that anything other than perfection is not good enough or not for public consumption… and that's a surefire recipe for stress and anxiety. It's why I share the good, the bad and the ugly of my own life in my podcast each week, because nobody is perfect. Be real, be raw, be you.

258. Actions speak louder than words.

When someone tells you they care and then repeatedly doesn't back it up with consistent actions, they're telling you loud and clear what you really need to know. Ask for what you need, call out behaviour that doesn't match words, and if it happens repeatedly then remove yourself from the situation. You are worth so much more. If someone treats you like an option, walk away.

259. Don't just 'go along' with things.

When I was younger I tried so hard to fit in, but the older I've gotten the more I've realised that just going along with what everyone else does takes you too far away from being your most honest and truthful self. And besides, when we just 'go along' with everything we end up forming mobs, so please don't let yourself end up as one of the torch-wielding villagers in a Frankenstein movie. Think for yourself.

260. Looks are less important than personality.

Your appearance really doesn't matter. Focus more on what others (and you) look like on the inside. Why? Because beauty fades, but kindness is eternal. I'm not going to feel bad for a physical trait that I have no direct control over. We need to worry less about what people look like and more about who they are. Pretty and shallow is still shallow, and looks fade. And it's better to be average-looking with a kind heart than pretty with an ugly heart. Be more than just your looks. Be kind and decent.

261. Happy people don't tear others to pieces.

Have you ever sat there listening to someone talk crap about someone else? That person is not happy. Happy people don't need to tear others to pieces to feel better about themselves; that's what miserable people do. People who feel happy and satisfied in life choose to let stuff just pass them by, instead of taking it on and internalising it and then gossiping or backstabbing. Remember that other peoples' stuff is about them, not you… and you can choose whether or not to engage.

262. If you feel cranky, take a break.

This bit of advice applies to arguments with others and also to any general feelings of crankiness you might have sometimes: when a child is cranky it usually needs a nap or something to eat, and honestly I find that the same thing works as an adult. The main point is to take a break rather than just running with the cranky feelings, because they will fade with time if you don't keep on giving them attention but if you act on them then you're probably going to cause a mess. If taking a break doesn't cut it for you, you could always just go sit in your car and scream it out… whatever works for you!

263. 1% beats 0%.

Sometimes there are days when I just don't have the energy — physically or emotionally — to do anything, however I know that doing nothing is going to make things feel worse for myself later, so if that happens I push myself to do just one small thing. That might mean putting away a couple of pieces of laundry instead of the whole basket, or tidying the coffee table instead of the whole room. Something is better than nothing, and sometimes it can also help you to find the energy to do a bit more than just that. And if not? Well, you've still done something — no matter how small!

264. Setting boundaries is uncomfortable.

The fact is that setting boundaries is tough, it's confronting, it's uncomfortable and it can even be painful. But that doesn't mean that you avoid it just because it's challenging, because boundaries are also necessary. When you've spent years allowing people to treat you however they want, setting and maintaining boundaries is going to feel weird and it's also probably going to bring up feelings of guilt at first. That happens because change is uncomfortable, even if that change is good for us. Push through the discomfort and keep going, because having healthy boundaries — and sticking to them — will absolutely change your life for the better.

265. Ageing is great.

I honestly never thought I'd say this, but I'm actually really enjoying the ageing process because there's a level of calm and peace of mind that comes with being able to put things into the broader context of your whole life; the older you are, the more you can begin to see the big picture and the less likely you are to get hung up on the little things. Having said that, your mindset is a choice and I've seen plenty of older people still bickering over nonsense that really doesn't matter… so remember that you get to choose how you live your life, and choosing a drama-free existence really does bring greater peace of mind.

266. Make your peace of mind a priority today.

When you consciously choose to prioritise calm and peace of mind, it has a direct effect on the choices you make as well as what you will and will not accept from others. It's easy to find ourselves caught up in all the day-to-day stuff that goes on, but by deciding to pursue your peace of mind above all things you'll find that a lot of the usual irritations and annoyances — the ones that might normally grab your attention and make your day feel stressful — will have much less of an impact on you. Go ahead, try it today!

267. Ask for what you need.

Most people don't get what they need because they don't ask for what they need; this may come as a surprise, but other people really cannot read your mind. Instead of expecting the people in your life to immediately know what you need, it's up to you to tell them in a kind and respectful way (and to ask what they need as well). These sorts of discussions can feel awkward at first, because we're so conditioned not to say these things, but the more you do it the easier and more comfortable it becomes. Try it today.

268. When we support others, they shine.

This applies to everyone, and especially to parents (plus it's very applicable in the workplace): when we support others they are able to shine, because they're not having to deal with worry or fear or whatever. It doesn't matter whether you agree with who someone else is or not; as long as they're not harming anyone, let them be themselves. That doesn't mean that you don't set healthy rules and boundaries, because they're still necessary (for everyone!), but it means that you choose not to project your own approach to life into others so that they can be 100% themselves, because that's when we're able to truly shine. There is no one 'correct' way to live.

269. Challenge your impostor syndrome.

Our doubts and fears can have us believing all sorts of things, questioning our abilities and even thinking that we're going to be 'found out' and ridiculed. Those thoughts are not facts; it's just your mind trying to protect you, although it's going a pretty messed-up way about it. Challenge that voice by reminding yourself of the truth: you are capable, and anything you're not confident with or competent in just yet can be learned through time, effort and perseverance. Do you think I knew what I was doing when I started my podcast? I had no idea! But I learned and I reminded myself daily that learning takes time, which helped to shut down my doubts and fears. Keep going.

270. Be curious.

Curiosity helps you to grow, and frankly I've come to realise that the older I get the less I really know… and that's totally fine. There is so much to discover in this world, more than could possibly fit into one lifetime, so choose to keep on learning a little every single day by asking questions and exploring new ideas. You're never done learning and I think that when we stop being curious we can find that life becomes dull and uninteresting… which is a shame, because life is anything but dull and uninteresting!

271. Give yourself space.

A while ago I took a couple of weeks off from doing my podcast and daily posts, because I was exhausted and running on auto-pilot. Within just a few days of giving myself permission to cut back on my responsibilities for two weeks, I suddenly found new ideas and approaches popping into my head seemingly out of nowhere… because when you give yourself space to just be, you're better able to tap into your creativity and you can then come up with new things to try instead of just running on the same hamster wheel over and over again.

272. You can leave toxic situations (and you should).

I saw something a while ago talking about how to deal with people that are potentially toxic, and as I said in my book *Let's Talk About Mental Health (Volume One)* you don't need to put up with crap. Whether it's a relationship or a job or whatever, give the other person a chance to change and meet you with kindness and respect, because that's how mature and healthy relationships work, but if that doesn't change things then it's time to move on. Like, now. Go on, I'll wait. Think of it this way: if you saw a big bottle marked 'toxic' would you repeatedly drink from it and then wonder why you're constantly getting sick? No! So don't do the same thing with people and situations. Prioritise your mental health and wellbeing. You will be OK.

273. Wherever you are, there you are.

It doesn't matter where you're at physically, it's where you're at mentally that matters the most. You could be in the most glamorous location in the world and feel absolutely miserable; your surroundings don't guarantee you a happily-ever-after. Do the work to feel good about where you're at inside, and the rest will follow with time, effort and perseverance.

274. Know when to try and when to say 'bye'.

There will always be challenging situations and relationships to deal with, and if you bail at the first sign of trouble then you'll never grow because confronting issues and dealing with them helps us to grow. But, at the same time, don't cling on long after the horse has bolted; learning when to let go enables you to look after your mental health and wellbeing, because sometimes the healthiest thing you can do is to walk away. If you've tried and it hasn't improved the situation, just remember this: nothing changes if nothing changes. Which means it might be time to move on.

275. 'No' is a complete sentence.

You are not required to justify your choices to anyone, so if you need to or want to say 'no' to a request then say no. End of sentence. You can do that with kindness and respect, and I do think that it's helpful to provide a little context in terms of explaining why, especially for people you're close with, because that can prevent misunderstandings and miscommunication... but you do not owe anyone an explanation, and that's the most important thing to remember. You get to decide what you do with your time and energy.

276. Mixed signals are a clear answer.

If you're not sure about how someone feels, ask them. And if you're getting evasiveness in return or if their words don't match their actions, there's your answer. Actions speak much louder than words, so never let someone treat you like an option. If you aren't being treated respectfully, call it out in a kind-yet-assertive way and then, if it doesn't change, move on. Remember: someone who is serious about you and who respects you will give you clarity, not confusion.

277. You get to decide what becomes of you.

This is a little bit similar to a piece of advice I gave earlier in the book which was "write your own story" and it's a handy little reminder that you are not defined by what happens to you; you are defined by what you choose to do with the things that have happened to you. Your challenges, your setbacks, your mistakes, your traumas… none of them have any power over you, because you are the one that has the ability to decide what happens next. So write a story for yourself where you triumph, because you can and you will.

278. Learn how to like yourself.

It's so easy to fall into the habit of worrying about what other people think about you, and whether or not they like you (I mean, that's basically the whole business model of social media!), but what matters more is whether or not *you* like you. When you genuinely like yourself — flaws and all — you then attract the right type of people into your life, and it's also much easier to let go of people who don't value you. Start by making a list of at least five things you like about yourself, and add one thing to it everyday.

279. Love is hard work.

If there's one thing I've learned from being with my partner for ages, it's just how much work it takes to build and maintain a mature relationship. The challenge is that relationships eventually move on from the initial 'fun and flirty' phase, where everything is excitement and lust and discovery, and when that mellows is when the work really begins; communicating, learning and growing together. A lot of people quit when it stops being fun but, with the right person, it can push you to grow and evolve as an individual. It's a challenge, but it's worth the work if it's a healthy relationship.

280. Focus on what you can control.

What other people do and say is their choice, how you respond is yours. You're never going to be able to control other people and the sooner you accept that and just focus on the choices you make, the easier it becomes to let go (especially if someone is treating you poorly). I may not be able to control what you say to me, but I can certainly control whether I let it get to me… and whether or not I give you another opportunity to do it again. And remember that it's not actually personal; what other people do and say is about them, and what's going on in their head.

281. Everything is a matter of perspective.

When I was a kid I used to think of teachers as being these all-knowing and all-powerful authority figures (and, I mean, they are; I have a huge respect for what teachers do) but they're just people going to work and doing their jobs… my partner teaches and seeing the behind-the-scenes makes you realise just how much everything in life is a matter of perspective, and how what you think is the truth is really just *your* truth, based on your worldview at that point in time. So, ask questions and look at the bigger picture so you can challenge your assumptions and build a broader perspective on life.

282. Lead with kindness.

There's plenty of negativity in this world and more than enough news outlets and social media accounts ready and willing to stir the pot and make things worse… choose not to get involved. Look, when given a choice between drama or no drama there's only one option that's going to bring you peace of mind and it ain't drama! You can't stop other people from being hateful, but you can most certainly stop yourself from being like that. Sometimes the kindest response is to just step back and step away rather than getting involved; let somebody else be involved in the drama instead of you.

283. Don't play it safe.

Never taking a risk might seem easier than exposing yourself to potential failure, but living involves trying new things and pushing yourself forward bit by bit. You'll never know if you never try, and really the worst that can happen is that you might fail — and that's OK, because it will teach you things that you can try for the next time. Playing it safe in life leads to feeling defeated later in life… don't let your future self down just because it feels a bit uncomfortable or scary to push yourself out of your comfort zone.

284. A 'good life' does not cost anything.

You really don't need diamonds rings or 18 carat gold to have a good life (and thanks to Madonna for that song line I just borrowed yet again!). Having the latest gadgets and taking luxury holidays might be fun, and I love my creature comforts as much as the next person, but what *really* makes life feel great is finding meaning and fulfilment in what you do and how you spend your time, taking small steps every day to grow, being surrounded by people who genuinely care for and support you, and finding peace of mind… and all of those things are completely free.

285. You can choose what you pay attention to.

I used to think that I was obligated to listen to the dramas of other people, and sometimes even let myself become caught up in them, until I finally realised one day that I have complete control over what I do and do not give my attention to. Now, I deliberately pull back at the first sign of drama and it has been the most liberating and freeing thing I've ever done in my life. When you let less drama in, you have less drama to deal with… sure, that sounds obvious but I think we forget that sometimes. It doesn't matter who the person is or how close they are to you; you can choose what you do or do not pay attention to and your choice shapes what happens next.

286. Find someone you can laugh with.

Whether it's a good friend or a partner, relationships based on a positive connection and an ability to genuinely have fun together are much healthier than ones based on more superficial things like looks or getting drunk together or whatever. With dating, especially, it's important to remember that the initial rush of excitement is going to eventually fade (because that's just what happens over time for most people) and so that's often when we discover the real person; if there's a genuine connection there, you can build something genuine together with time, effort and perseverance. Besides, looks fade… but laughter is forever.

287. Know the difference between optimism and delusion.

I am quite optimistic and I genuinely believe that most things will turn out for the best… but I also balance that mindset with reality. That means I make sure that I balance my thought processes with a realistic assessment of things and I don't allow myself to let wishful thinking distract me from the truth. For example, there are some people in my life who aren't really the nicest people and so rather than giving them chance after chance to change (when it's clear that they don't want to), I accept that all I can change is myself and so I keep my distance. Don't let hope distract you from making healthy choices based on reality.

288. Notice your emotions.

Oftentimes we just react to our emotions without really stopping to think about where they're coming from or what they might actually be trying to tell us. I want to encourage you to try this: for the next two weeks, every time you have a strong emotional response to something I want you to pause, notice the emotion, breathe through it for at least 10 seconds, and then ask yourself what you're feeling and why… and then, make a note of it every single time. After a week or two you should begin to see patterns emerging that tell you more about where your emotional reactions come from; use that information to start addressing the root of your emotions so that you can stop reacting and, instead, begin responding more thoughtfully.

289. Upgrade your habits.

You can't expect new results from old behaviours, so if you want to create change in your life then *you* need to create change in your life. That can feel really overwhelming and often we don't really know where to start, so here's what I suggest: pick one small thing this week and focus on it. That could be as simple as committing to five minutes a day of gentle stretching (and then actually doing it). As you become more comfortable you can slowly build on it over the following week, and again the week after that. Small changes can add up over time to big results, and it starts with the choices you make today.

290. Your words have power.

The next time you feel annoyed, irritated, hurt, upset, or just plain angry, remember that what you say to do shapes what happens next… so choose not to let those kinds of intense emotions create more problems for your future self. Instead of snapping or clapping back, choose to pause and let your emotions calm down so that you can choose your words and actions more thoughtfully. Your words and actions have the power to shape what happens next, and so when you remember that fact then you can be much more conscious about the path you're choosing to create for yourself.

291. You are not your past.

Most of us, if not all of us, have things that have happened in our past which may be upsetting, hurtful or even traumatic… but those things do not define you; it's what you choose to do with your past that defines you. Your ability to confront your demons and take away their power is what helps you to find ways to move forward with confidence, knowledge and strength, and if you need some help doing that then work with a counsellor or therapist who you feel comfortable with. You are not your past; you are what you choose to do with your past. Let it be the fuel that propels you forward into a better future.

292. Make the most of every day.

Each day really is a gift and so we should be celebrating it, rather than focusing on what may or may not happen in the future. That doesn't mean that you need to wake up tomorrow and climb a mountain or go and paint your own version of the Sistine Chapel, but you *can* choose to make the most of every day simply by committing to being fully present and enjoying each day to the fullest, regardless of what you're doing. It's less about what you're doing and more about *how* you're doing it; are you truly living each day, or are you just existing? The choice is yours.

293. Judge less, love more.

When you choose not to judge other people you create more space for kindness. Everybody has their own things that they're dealing with in life and we don't need to add judgement on top of all of that. Of course we're not all going to agree on how or why things are done, but as long as someone else isn't doing any harm to you, others or themselves, just leave them be; that's kindness in action, and kindness is love. And when we replace judgement with love, we change the world one interaction at a time.

294. Even the people you love are not perfect.

You don't have to love everything about someone in order to love them; we all have flaws, and I'm sure there are things about you that annoy them just as much as there are things about them that annoy you! Love is accepting people for who they are, flaws and all, and being willing to love them even if and when they drive you up the wall. Provided a relationship is based on mutual kindness and respect, then it's a healthy one… so don't feel bad about getting annoyed sometimes, because you're only human.

295. Love is not a magic cure.

There's this common fairytale ending to movies and TV shows where love seems to be all that someone needs to overcome obstacles and deal with their challenges, and that just isn't true; love provides you with necessary support and the feeling of being cared for, but it doesn't 'fix' your issues because only time, effort and perseverance can do that. So remember that love of any kind — family, friends, partner, whatever — cannot be the thing that you pin all your hopes on to 'cure' all of your problems, because life doesn't work like that. *You* need to do the work; the support will help, but it doesn't replace the work.

296. Complaining is negative energy.

Look, I get it… sometimes we all just feel annoyed about something and we need to have a bit of a moan to let off some steam. But when complaining becomes a habit that's when it can cause you harm; instead of focusing on problems, choose to focus on solutions because what you focus on is what you focus on. No amount of complaining will ever change your circumstances; only positive action can create positive change.

297. To love is to live.

Of all the possible ways to describe what life is all about, I have to believe that it all comes back to love. Put simply, loving is living; it is our purest expression of what it means to be human, and it is our capacity to love and be loved that defines our existence. When you choose to love more you are choosing to live more, and it also helps to let all the other stuff — the things that really just don't matter — fade into the background, which is where they belong. Loving is the true purpose of life.

298. Look for the lesson.

When stuff happens in our life, especially the not-so-great stuff, it might be tempting to wonder, "Why is this happening to me?" But the *real* question — the one that can help you to make peace with things — is, "What can this teach me?" Look, of course we don't want to have unpleasant experiences in life however we cannot control everything. So, when faced with tough times we can regain our control by turning our attention back to the one thing we can always do: consciously choosing to learn from any situation, good or bad. That's what helps you to move forward.

299. Let go of expectation.

Any time I've been really specific about what I expect to happen or to receive, I've usually been disappointed because the reality doesn't match my expectations. However, when you learn how to set broad hopes and aspirations, and then allow life to surprise you with the results, you're better able to see opportunities and possibilities. There are many different ways to achieve the same outcome; instead of getting hung up on the specifics of the 'how' instead allow yourself to consider what you want, broadly speaking, and why.

300. Less 'should' and more 'could'.

The word 'should' is so heavily-laden with judgement — you *should* be doing this, it *shouldn't* be this hard, I *should* be good at this — however the fact is that you can 'should' all you like but all it's going to do is make you feel bad about yourself… and who wants to live like that?! Instead, choose to focus on 'could': what *could* you do? What are the options available to you that are within your control? When you redirect your focus from judgements to positivity, you change the way you look at yourself and the world.

301. Spend time with people who lift you up.

There are some people who will happily try to tear you to pieces or drag you down to their level; maybe they do it deliberately, because they're miserable, or maybe they do it subconsciously, because they're not self-aware. Whether they intend to drag you down or not is irrelevant, because the result is the same: you'll find your energy and positivity being drained. Instead of allowing that to happen, choose to limit your time around those people and don't get too invested in their baggage, and instead choose to spend your time with positive people who are kind and supportive. It will make life much more pleasant.

302. Truth is better than deceit.

Given a choice between hearing what I want to hear and hearing what I need to hear, I'd rather hear the truth; it might not always feel comfortable and it might be confronting, but knowing the truth is better than believing lies. The same goes for how you interact with others; instead of avoiding the truth to protect someone's feelings, it's better to be honest. You can do that with kindness and respect, and it's much healthier than deception. And please remember that not saying anything is also a form of deception.

303. Let go of what might have been.

You know that thing you think about sometimes that could have played out differently if only you had done this or that instead? You're torturing yourself. What has happened has happened; you cannot change the past, and by constantly thinking about what might have been you are just keeping yourself stuck in regret. Instead, choose to make your peace with whatever happened (or didn't happen) and give yourself permission to move forward with acceptance, trust, hope, optimism, and a large dose of self-kindness. You can't change what might have been yesterday, but you can definitely create what may be tomorrow.

304. Be proactive about your mental health.

It's easy to forget that your mental health needs regular care and attention, just like your physical health does; I hate to break it to you, but your mental health isn't going to just take care of itself! Pick a few things you enjoy doing for yourself and do them every day: mindfulness, gratitude practice, journaling, quiet time outdoors, reading, connecting with people you care about… there are countless ways to look after your mental health (and I cover lots of ideas in my weekly podcast), so choose what works for you. The main thing is to do something and do it daily… because if you don't look after your mental health, then who will?!

305. Make kindness your default.

In a world full of nastiness and cruelty, you can either choose to be nasty as well or you can choose to be kind; the fact is that two wrongs don't make a right, and so when you choose to lead with kindness you're choosing to do no harm… and every choice you make, no matter how small, shapes what happens next. Be kind to yourself (because life is challenging enough without being mean to yourself!), and be kind to others, because most people are dealing with stuff you will never know about or understand, so giving them even just a little kindness can make an enormous difference. And if you can't do that, just leave them be; neutral is better than negative! Kindness for the win.

306. Be different.

Sometimes I scroll through Instagram and my eyes roll into the back of my head because there are *so* many people doing the same thing over and over again. Why? Given a choice between being the same or being different, I'll choose different every single day of the week because it's more interesting and it's more honest; we're all unique, so allow yourself to be your unique and authentic self. I don't know about you but I have zero interest in being like everyone else; I tried doing that when I was younger and it just made me miserable. I'm far more content now just being my true self, and not following what everyone else is doing.

307. All experiences can teach you something.

Things won't always go to plan and that's OK, because life is about learning; sometimes you get what you want, and sometimes you get what you need. Every situation has something to teach you, even if that thing is what you don't want or what not to do in future, and the fact is that if life were 'happy happy, joy joy' all the time then we'd never be challenged to push ourselves to grow… and imagine how boring life would be if we never grew?! The purpose of life is to grow and to slowly become the best version of yourself possible, so look for what each experience is trying to teach you and learn what you need to learn so that you can grow.

308. Trust your instincts.

When you get a really strong feeling about something, don't ignore it; that's your soul trying to talk to you, and I've found that ignoring it usually results in a big old mess. There is scientific evidence that suggests people who follow their hunches tend to have better results than those who ignore them, so learn how to tune into what your body is telling you. Listen to your instincts and let them guide you, and use rational thought to help you find the balance between emotion and logic so you can make a smart and considered choice.

309. Most of your worries will never happen.

We often spend so much time worrying about things that we forget to take a step back and look at the actual likelihood of whether or not they will really ever eventuate; frankly, you have a higher chance of winning the lottery than you do of having the things you worry about come true! Instead of letting worry distract you, choose to notice those thoughts and label them as your brain trying to protect you, then thank your brain for its efforts and tell it that you're OK and safe. That way you'll find it easier to calm yourself (instead of trying to resist the thoughts, which rarely works) and you can just let those worried thoughts pass by you with ease. Remember: thoughts are not facts.

310. Enjoy your own company.

I used to struggle being on my own (which is kind-of funny because I'm an only child, so you'd think I'd be used to it!) and it took me a long time to realise that I found it difficult because I'd spent so long running from who I really was. When you learn to love yourself for who you really are, you find it easier to really enjoy your own company and that gives you an opportunity to experience moments of quiet reflection which can then help you to recharge your batteries. We all need a bit of 'me time' to rest and recharge, and to connect with our true selves.

311. Don't overthink things.

Sometimes you just have to take a chance; you're never going to have it all figured out anyway, and so if you wait until the time is right or until everything is perfect then you'll be waiting for eternity… and that's just a waste of a good life. Look, you do need to think about things a little bit so that you don't just jump into everything without any thought (because that usually makes a mess of things!), but don't let yourself get into 'analysis paralysis'; overthinking robs you of joy and it just bogs you down in worry. When in doubt, just give it a go and see what happens.

312. Everyone's priorities are different.

We each have our own idea of what matters most and that's OK; this world would be a very boring place if we were all the same, and it's our diversity and creativity that defines us as a human race. No single person or group of people is better than another, and just because something matters to you that doesn't mean everyone will share your viewpoint. Do no harm and be kind, and choose to find common ground with people instead of arguing over different perspectives.

313. What you say and do shapes the world.

Every choice you make, every word you speak and every action you take has a ripple effect, not only on your life but also the lives of those around you… and so it also slowly ripples out into the world, little by little. Great change happens one tiny step at a time, and you can choose to be a part of positive change simply by being thoughtful about what you do and say. Want to help change the world? Start by sharing kind opinions, and keeping unkind opinions to yourself.

314. Don't believe everything you think.

Our brains have a magnificent capacity for drama and catastrophising things, especially if you live with anxiety or other conditions because that means your brain is in a heightened state of alert more often which leads it to spend a lot of time worrying or ruminating (or both). However the truth is that thoughts are not facts; they're just thoughts, and they're not necessarily true. Instead of allowing your thoughts to distract you and make you feel stressed or anxious, you can choose to just let them gently pass like clouds in the sky.

315. What are you waiting for?

We spend so much time throughout our lives waiting for the conditions to be perfect, but they never will be because life doesn't work like that. So, don't put off until tomorrow what you need to or want to do today. Your future is created by the choices that you make today, so if you want to create a future you feel proud of then it requires you to push past fear and find the courage to take one small step today, followed by another, and then another. Progress is made through each choice you make, so don't waste your time wasting your time.

316. You are more than your work.

We all have to work to earn a living, but what you do to pay the bills doesn't define who you are as a human being and it certainly doesn't contain the meaning of life. I think that 'What do you do for a living?' is the worst question in the world, because it reinforces this idea that's developed over the past century or so that we're defined by what we do to earn money. We're not. Life is about living, loving and finding meaning… sure, you can do that while you work, but there's so much more to life than the job you do. Live your life to its fullest and work to live instead of living to work. Your work is not your worth.

317. Trust yourself.

You know you better than anyone knows you, you know?! Seriously, why do we second-guess ourselves so often when we are the only person in the entire world who knows every single little detail of who we are and who we are not? Instead of doubting yourself, take the time to really get to know yourself so that you can trust yourself. That sense of self-trust leads to less self-doubt and more self-confidence, and it can help you to conquer any challenge you're faced with.

318. 'What If?' is a dangerous game.

It's human nature to sometimes think about the past and consider what might have been if we did this or that instead… but when you do that, you take yourself down a path of rumination and regret which isn't particularly helpful or healthy. The healthier way to approach it is to consider this question: "What can I learn from that situation, and what could I do differently if I'm faced with something similar in the future?" By doing that, your focus is on moving forward with self-compassion and kindness rather than being filled with regrets over a past that you can never change anyway. What's done is done; learn from it and move forward.

319. Eyes forward.

Have you ever had a time where you haven't been paying full attention to where you're going and you've walked into a door or a wall? That happened to me once on vacation and I spent a few days with a very painful bruised rib, which not surprisingly made it hard to enjoy myself. The point I'm making here is that when you focus on where you're heading, instead of looking back over your shoulder, you're more likely to see obstacles coming your way so you can avoid them or minimise the damage. Stop looking backwards… you're not going that way.

320. Nobody has all the answers.

We're all just making things up as we go along and there isn't a single person on this planet who has it all figured out (and if someone tells you they do, they're full of crap). I am very open about the fact that I, like Jon Snow from *Game of Thrones*, know nothing… I mean I know *something*, otherwise I wouldn't be able to function, but you get my point. The journey of life involves learning, and the more you learn the more you realise just how many more questions there are to be answered… and that's the joy of life, the figuring out. Take your time and enjoy the process.

321. See the bigger picture.

I hate to break it to you, but your life is just one tiny part of an infinitely enormous tapestry. That's a good thing, because it helps you to see that your day-to-day problems really aren't as big as they might seem in the moment, and I find comfort in knowing that I'm part of something much greater than just my own existence; that's actually what helps me to find meaning and purpose in my life, by feeling part of something bigger (side note: my favourite thing to do is stare at the stars on a clear night, because it reminds me of just how enormous this universe of ours truly is). And the best part is that we can all contribute something positive to this bigger picture, just by virtue of the choices we make each day.

322. Talking helps.

I have days where I can feel stressed or overwhelmed by my emotions, and I find that it really helps to talk with someone I trust instead of bottling up my feelings; if you don't let it out then it stays inside, and it can build and build and build until you're ready to explode. Sometimes a good stress rant is all you need; I find it helps to let the other person know that I need to vent and ask if they'd just listen while I run out of steam; I'm usually not looking for solutions from them, but instead I just need a willing and sympathetic ear so I can release all that energy in order to then focus on finding my own solutions. Journalling can help with this too. Let it out to get it out.

323. Push past fear.

Fear is a perfectly natural response to keep us safe from lions and tigers and bears (oh my!), but it's not terribly helpful when it holds us back from trying new things in order to grow and achieve our goals in life. Recognise that fear is your brain's way of trying to keep you safe, so thank it for doing so and then let it know that you're OK and that you want to try new things one step at a time. Remember that all of your hopes and dreams live on the other side of fear, so don't let it hold you back.

324. Change your attitude, change your future.

I almost feel like this one sounds a bit like an infomercial ("try all-new positive attitude and change your entire life!"), but the fact remains that if you choose to refocus your attitude and mindset towards hope, optimism, kindness and solutions then you're going to steer yourself in a much more positive direction than if you give all of your energy to negativity. And do you know what? It feels better! I don't know about you, but I find negative energy completely draining. When you focus on cultivating a positive attitude, you create a positive future for yourself.

325. What matters to you is up to you.

We're fed all of these messages throughout our lives about what should matter and what shouldn't, but the fantastic thing about being a unique human being is that you get to decide what truly matters to you; if you give something value then it has value, and if you decide something isn't important then it isn't important. It all comes down to the choices you make. So… what *really* matters to you? For me it's peace of mind, my loved ones, and doing work that feels genuinely meaningful to me. What about you? If you're not sure, start by asking yourself what *doesn't* matter to you and then work from there.

326. Keep going.

There will be days you feel tired. Keep going. There will be days where it all feels like too much. Keep going. There will be days when you doubt yourself and you question your abilities. Keep going. Progress is made with time, effort and perseverance. When you plant a seed, it takes time for it to break through the surface and begin to reach for the sky in order to fulfil its potential. Don't just give up if things are taking time to develop and grow, because all of that effort and perseverance will pay off in time if you just focus on one step at a time and keep going. When in doubt, always choose to keep going!

327. You have more than one purpose.

We seem to have this idea that we have to find the one specific thing that is meant just for us, and my issue with that idea is that it's a very narrow way of looking at the world and at life in general. I'm doing work now that feels meaningful and purposeful to me, but the same was true years ago when I worked in the corporate sector (I mean, not all of my jobs in corporate; some of them were horrendous!). The point is that you grow over time and so I think it's healthy to focus on trying lots of different things and allowing yourself the space to evolve, rather than buying into the idea that we have to find the one specific thing that will define us for the rest of our lives.

328. What you nurture will flourish.

I'm not great at gardening — I've even managed to kill a cactus more than once in the past — but my partner is good at it, and I've noticed that when you do the work and really care for a plant it will prosper; on the other hand, when you neglect it then it will wither and die. We human beings are the same. When we feel neglected we don't do very well, but when we are nourished and cared for we can absolutely thrive. You need to be the one who nurtures yourself and meets your own needs, and it's the choices you make that will determine how well you flourish; so, be thoughtful and choose wisely.

329. Move forward.

The things that happened, the people that hurt you, the mistakes made, the opportunities missed… it's all in the past. You can choose to let it haunt you here in the present, or you can let it go and leave it in the past. It has no power over you now unless you give it power, and so it can't hurt you unless you let it. That doesn't mean that what happened was OK; it simply means that you realise that acceptance is necessary to move forward, and that moving forward is how you find peace of mind.

330. You can't compare the past and the present.

The author L. P. Hartley once wrote, "the past is a foreign country: they do things differently there," and it's an excellent reminder that we really cannot compare the past and the present. You made the choices you made back then based on who you were at that time and what you knew then; of course you know more now, because we learn over time, and so maybe you would have made different choices... but frankly that's wasted energy to even think about. What is is what is, and no amount of going over it will ever change that fact. Instead of regret and shame, give yourself kindness and compassion... and stop comparing that older version of you to the person you are today.

331. Some people don't want to change.

One of the hardest things in life is when you know someone who is making an absolute mess of their lives but they don't see anything wrong, kind of like that cartoon dog in the meme where he sits in the middle of the house while it's on fire saying, "this is fine." Not all people want to change, even when it's an opportunity to heal and get better. Why? Because change is scary, and some people will choose the safety and comfort of the familiar over the fear and uncertainty of the unknown — even if the familiar is toxic and unhealthy. All you can do is accept people as they are, or let the relationship go. You cannot make someone change, especially if they have no interest in changing.

332. Mental illness sucks... but it's not the end of the world.

Dealing with challenges with your mental health, like anxiety or depression, can be exhausting, but it's also an opportunity to discover a new way of being. Mental illness happens for a variety of reasons, but the main thing is that it's a sign something needs to change in your life in order to address the root cause of whatever is happening. That can be scary, sure, but it means you're being encouraged to let go of the things that no longer serve you in order to make way for the new... and so even the darkest of times can be an opportunity to grow something new and amazing.

333. Curate your feed, curate your life.

You get to choose who and what gets your attention, and so if there are people online or in the real world who make you feel bad about yourself then unfollow them or minimise your exposure to them. Whatever you focus on is what you focus on, so instead of allowing yourself to be distracted by negativity choose to focus your energy towards positive and constructive people.

334. Satisfaction is the new successful.

Give me a choice between a shiny new car and a life that feels calm and satisfying, I'm taking the way my life feels over stuff any day of the week. I feel like we've spent so many years being told that it's our material wealth that determines how successful we are, and it took me a long time to figure out that it's actually our emotional wealth that leads to true success in life. And that doesn't mean you need to reject money and live in poverty; it just means that you choose to prioritise your peace of mind over 'stuff' that you can't take with you anyway.

335. It's not the clothes, it's the spirit.

It doesn't matter what you look like or what you wear, what matters is who you are and how you make your way through this world. If you choose to do no harm, are kind, and you give more than you take, then you are one of the most beautiful people on the face of this planet… and never let anything or anyone take that away from you. We need more people in this world who lead with kindness and compassion!

336. Don't follow trends, set them.

If you do the same as what everyone else is doing then you're just blending in and, honestly, isn't that a bit dull? Like, really?! Out of all of the billions of us on this planet you're telling me that you want to be *exactly* the same as a massive bunch of people?! Instead of trying to fit in and do what everyone else is doing, be your true and authentic self. It's definitely a lot more fun!

337. Slowing down is freedom.

Choosing to create space for yourself in your life is true freedom. When you identify your priorities and make them your main focus, you begin to realise how much stuff that really doesn't matter takes up your headspace every day. Letting go of what doesn't matter is where true personal freedom is to be found.

338. Be kind, but don't put up with crap.

'Being kind' doesn't mean 'being a doormat' and so if people are working your last nerve or pushing your boundaries, you need to make that stop. Do so in a kind and fair way, but be firm and assertive. If you allow crap to continue, you will wind up dealing with more crap.

339. Stop blaming others for your problems.

Instead of looking for someone else to blame, begin by honestly assessing your role in things. We are each responsible for the choices we make in life, and since nobody can force us to do or say anything that's where your focus and energy needs to be. When you try to shift the blame externally, instead of taking ownership and holding yourself accountable for the choices you make, all you're doing is taking yourself further and further away from facing the truth and making the changes you need to make. It's your life, so act like it and take responsibility for your actions.

340. Kindness does not equal nice.

You don't have to be 'nice' to be kind; just don't be cruel. The idea of 'being nice' is an old-fashioned notion that basically involves putting up with crap so as not to rock the boat. I am not nice, although I am kind (most of the time… unless you push me, then I will turn like a cut snake!). Being 'nice' usually leads to not tackling issues if and when they arise, which leads to resentment and frustration building over time, and that's just not healthy. My two general rules for being kind are: don't be a dick, but also don't put up with crap.

341. Don't vent to others.

If you have an issue with someone, talk to them directly instead of involving other people in the issue, because that just creates unnecessary drama… and drama creates the opposite of peace of mind. If you have difficulty talking to someone about issues or you find the idea of confrontation terrifying or uncomfortable, take some time to plan what you need to say and maybe even have a 'practice run' with a friend or colleague before you tackle the real conversation. It's much healthier than venting in a non-constructive way.

342. Sometimes you need a 'people-free' day.

Some people draw energy from being around others, whereas other people need some time to themselves to recharge and recover after spending time with people. I'm in the latter group, especially since I spend five days a week working with people in what is emotionally-intensive work. Introverts in particular need time to themselves on a regular basis; it took me a long time to work out that I'm actually an introvert (I used to think I was an extrovert, but it turns out I'm an introvert who has a whole bunch of trauma around rejection and so I was constantly seeking the approval of others which made me try to behave like an extrovert!). Even if you're not someone who thrives on time to yourself, be kind and understanding to your friends and loved ones who might need some solo time every now and then to recharge.

343. Don't cling onto things.

Clinging on to something or someone isn't healthy; it's a desperate act. You know that saying, "clinging on for dear life"? That's a pure survival instinct and it doesn't involve thinking about what is right for you, it's just about trying to survive. Sometimes you need to let go, like the trees let go of their leaves as the seasons change — and no amount of clinging on will ever make the leaves stay. Let go with grace and dignity, and know that you will land on your feet.

344. Feelings are not permanent.

Allow yourself to feel your feelings, but know that they won't be with you for forever… which is a good thing. Feelings are like clouds slowly drifting across the sky; one moment they're there, the next they're gone. Don't try to deny your feelings, because that tends to make them more likely to hover around (not a good thing when you don't feel great), but instead just observe them and consider what they have to teach you about what really matters most to you, and then let them pass gently by with grace and ease.

345. Relationships require work.

All relationships — romantic, friendships, family, work colleagues, that neighbour you nod to every now and then — require consistent effort if they are to survive and thrive, otherwise they'll wither and wilt over time like a neglected houseplant. If a relationship matters to you then do the work.

346. Just because you can, that doesn't mean you should.

We all have so many options available to us, which is a wonderful thing, but we need to stop just acting on our emotional impulses and instead take a few moments to think about what we're doing first. Choices have consequences and I would rather take a few minutes to think about whether or not I'm making a healthy and smart decision that's going to be in line with my priorities and set me up for future success, instead of just doing or saying things without thinking and then creating a mess I need to clean up later. Not everything is in your best interests.

347. Let things be what they are.

A lot of our frustration and unhappiness comes from trying to make things into what we believe they should be, rather than accepting them for what they are and then moving forward from there. 'Acceptance' does not mean that you like something or endorse it; it simply means you stop resisting reality so that you can then work with what is, rather than wasting energy wishing things were different. Wishes don't create change, action does. And to create effective and sustainable action you need to focus on what is, rather than what you wish it were, so you can then do the work to create the change you desire.

348. Keep your work life and personal life separate.

We spend a huge amount of time working and yet it can be hard for us to accept that our work life is not our real life, and so we need to think about how we set and maintain boundaries between the two. Work is what pays your bills to feed your belly; your home life is what feeds your soul. It's healthy to keep a distance between the two in order to ensure your identity doesn't become completely wrapped up in what you do for a living. Why? Because circumstances change. Companies downsize, great bosses leave and you wind up with terrible bosses, market forces change the way the business operates… there are so many external forces at work that are out of your control, and the one truth in life is that nothing is permanent, so remember that you need to make you your number one priority in order to look after your wellbeing in the long term.

349. You are never going to have it all figured out.

This world is so vast and there is so much to learn, and frankly it's just not possible to learn it all in a hundred lifetimes… let alone one! To find peace of mind you need to accept that you cannot ever figure it all out. That might sound overwhelming or even scary to comprehend, but it actually leads to a sense of relief when you finally accept it… because instead of constantly feeling like you have to have it all figured out, you can then allow yourself to be a lifelong learner and just enjoy the journey.

350. Stop avoiding conflict.

If you have an issue with someone, say something to them. Don't wait for things to magically fix themselves because they don't just fix themselves, and issues have a tendency to snowball into problems, which then become major problems, and the next thing you know you have a monumental mess on your hands that you have no idea how to deal with. I know conflict can be uncomfortable, but healthy conflict is necessary if we're to find middle ground.

351. Be where you are.

Sometimes we can become so fixated on how we feel about the place that we're currently at in life that we lose sight of the fact that wherever you are is where you are; you cannot change the past, only the future. So, take the time to learn why you are where you are and then do what you need to do to create the future you actually want. You are in control of your destiny at all times.

352. Time does not equal satisfaction.

We seem to think that sticking with something for the long term will eventually lead us to feel happy about it, even if it's not healthy for us, but it won't. Staying in a job you hate or a relationship that makes you unhappy is wasted energy; it's not going to magically get better. You can put in the work to try to improve it, but some things aren't improvable and so you need to know when to cut your losses. Never stay in a situation that is unhealthy or unsatisfying; do what you can to improve it, and if that doesn't work then remove yourself from the situation and move forward with your life.

353. Learn how to be patient with yourself.

All great things in life take time; mountains are not built overnight, so why are you expecting yourself to achieve everything in the blink of an eye? Stop putting so much pressure on yourself and give yourself time to grow and evolve into the very best version of yourself possible, someone who knows that the journey of personal growth keeps on going for the rest of your life. When you show yourself patience and compassion, you'll be able to make positive changes in your life in a more sustainable way.

354. Seek out new experiences.

It's easy to fall into a pattern of doing the same thing all the time, because it's familiar and familiarity is comfortable. But comfort doesn't help you to grow. I don't think you should throw out things that are safe and familiar, but do I think that all things in life involve balance and so if you just spend every single day doing the same thing over and over again then eventually you'll find yourself bored out of your head. Try new things and expand your mind, because that helps you to feel like you're growing and evolving.

355. Take your time.

You don't have to do all the things immediately, and it's OK to take things one step at a time — in fact, it's recommended. Consciously living at a slower pace enables you to be more thoughtful about what you do and how you do it, and it affords you the time you need to savour the little things in life… because they're actually the things that matter the most.

356. Listen to your heart.

Besides being a classic 90's song by Roxette, 'listen to your heart' is one of the most important pieces of advice you can ever receive. Why? Because your heart knows what truly matters to you and what you really want out of life, both for yourself and for the people you care for the most, so when you find yourself unsure of where to turn or what to do next, find some quietness and listen to your heart. It knows.

357. Energy attracts energy.

Negative energy attracts negative energy. Positive energy attracts positive energy. That means that what you choose to put out is what will make its way back to you, and that whether you choose to look for the negative or for the positive, what you seek is what you will find… so choose wisely. If you ever find yourself dealing with negativity, consciously turn your focus towards positivity instead. This is also a good time to remind you that you can — and should — choose to remove negative influences from your life.

358. What other people do is about them, not you.

Even if you're kind to others, it's an unfortunate fact of life that you may not always receive that same energy in return. Don't let that deter you from being kind; just remove those types of people from your life. If someone treats you poorly, that's 100% about them and their issues. Let go and move forward. There are plenty of people in the world who will love you for who you are.

359. Read more, learn more.

Aside from reading being fundamental (thanks, RuPaul), reading allows you to expand your mind and learn about new ideas and concepts that you might never have been exposed to. Non-fiction books serve to educate you and help you to see new possibilities, and fiction books allow you to be swept away by your imagination and the world created by the author. Either way, you're learning every time you read… so, read as much as you can (or at least a little every day!).

360. Make time for your wellbeing daily.

Your wellbeing is 100% your responsibility. Yes, you read that right… 100% *your* responsibility. Nobody can do it for you; they can certainly contribute positively, but they cannot do the actual work involved in looking after your wellbeing. It's up to you to make your wellbeing a priority and to actually look after yourself. Even just a few minutes a day will make an enormous difference, although I would definitely encourage you to allow more time than that since it's so important for your quality of life and overall health!

361. Stop doing things that harm yourself.

You know exactly what I'm talking about when I say 'things that harm yourself' — it's the habits and behaviours that you do on a regular basis which you know aren't in your best interests, yet you do them anyway… stop. You are harming yourself in the long term. And the same goes for allowing harmful relationships in your life. Don't. You get to choose who has access to you, and what that access looks and feels like. If it causes you any kind of harm, tell them and give them an opportunity to stop. If they don't, revoke their access to you. End of sentence.

362. Don't be your own bully.

Sometimes the cruelest person in our lives is ourselves. Actually, I'd say it's a lot more often than just 'sometimes' because we can tend to be really tough on ourselves and hold ourselves to impossibly-high standards. Why would you choose to go through life making yourself feel bad about yourself? This is why I continue to work with a therapist on an ongoing basis, because it allows me to work through self-esteem and self-compassion issues so I can be kinder to myself. Stop being your own worst enemy.

363. Create balance in all things.

Night and day, light and dark, yin and yang, work and home, wake and sleep. Everything in life is about finding a healthy balance for yourself, one that enables you to enjoy the highs while also being able to manage the lows (which are unavoidable). Take the time to think about what the idea of finding balance means to you and look at how you can make your own sense of balance a priority.

364. Breathe.

In 1998 the wise philosopher Kylie Minogue advised us to, "breathe, breathe… it won't be long now" and she was onto some good advice there, because taking a few moments to just calmly breathe allows you to reset your emotions and it gives time for your thoughts to pass like clouds in the sky. Nothing is permanent, so if you feel stressed or overwhelmed then just close your eyes and gently breathe for a minute to allow yourself time to calm and refocus.

365. Growth is a choice.

Growth doesn't just happen by virtue of going about your business every day; you have to make a conscious choice that you need to and want to grow, and then you have to do the work. And let me tell you this: the work is tough, it's gruelling, it's exhausting and there will be days where you just want to scream at everyone and everything to just leave you be… but then, when you look back for a moment and see just how far you've come by choosing to do the work in order to grow a little every day, that's when you realise that growth is a choice you have to make — and keep on making — because you are deserving of being the best version of yourself possible. Choose growth above all things, even when it's uncomfortable.

BONUS: Don't be a dick.

Sure, I could have just left this at 365 bits of *Life Advice That Doesn't Suck*... but how could I possibly finish this book without giving you my favourite piece of advice of all time?! We do tend to overcomplicate things quite a lot and I think life is a simple proposition: choose to do no harm, be kind and give more than you take (and I'm referring to how you treat others and how you treat yourself there). And, when in doubt, just remember not to be a dick and you'll be fine.

About the Author

Jeremy Godwin was born in Sydney, Australia in 1976 and moved to Melbourne, Australia in 2001. In 2011 he experienced a total breakdown, followed by several years of severe depression and anxiety, and in 2015 made the move from the city to a small country town in southern New South Wales, Australia. He spent several years completing a tertiary degree in sociology and psychology, as a means of trying to better understanding his own experiences with mental health challenges, and that eventually led him to start the *Let's Talk About Mental Health* podcast in late 2019 in order to create the kind of content he had difficulty finding during his own darkest moments. Now Jeremy focuses on sharing simple and practical tools for better mental health each week, delivered in his customary blunt-but-caring way.

Jeremy lives in a small cottage with his partner, two cats and four chickens, watched over by his beloved Spice Girls dolls as he works in his home office each day. He may or may not have an addiction to coffee (black), and enjoys finding new and inventive ways to incorporate pop culture references from the past several decades into his work.

Other Works by Jeremy Godwin

For more content, check out these offerings by Jeremy Godwin

Book: *Let's Talk About Mental Health (Volume One)*, available from Amazon and Apple Books

Podcast: *Let's Talk About Mental Health*, new episodes every Sunday (visit www.letstalkaboutmentalhealth.com.au for details)

And find Jeremy on Instagram @jeremygodwinofficial (you can also follow the *Let's Talk About Mental Health* podcast @ltamentalhealth)

Printed in Great Britain
by Amazon

16199321R00220